Wishing on the Midnight Star

Wishing on the Midnight Star

My Asperger Brother

Nancy Ogaz

Jessica Kingsley Publishers
London and New York

The right of Nancy Ogaz to be identified as author of this work has been asserted by her in accordance with the Copyright, Designs and Patents Act 1988.

First published in the United Kingdom in 2004
by Jessica Kingsley Publishers Ltd
116 Pentonville Road
London N1 9JB, England
and
29 West 35th Street, 10th fl.
New York, NY 10001–2299, USA

www.jkp.com

Copyright © Nancy Ogaz 2004

Library of Congress Cataloging in Publication Data
A CIP catalog record for this book is available from the Library of Congress

British Library Cataloguing in Publication Data
A CIP catalogue record for this book is available from the British Library

ISBN 1 84310 757 0

Printed and Bound in Great Britain by
Athenaeum Press, Gateshead, Tyne and Wear

Dedicated to my son, Cory

Contents

Acknowledgements

Many people, in many different ways, have contributed to the development and completion of this book.

Paula Jacobsen was very generous with her time and gave many thoughtful insights. Rita Ritchie, my instructor at the Institute for Children's Literature, guided me through each step of this manuscript with wisdom and extreme patience. Jessica Kingsley helped enormously with her honest suggestions (and, of course, subsequent acceptance for publication). Pauline Phillips steered me down the homestretch of this book. I owe you all much appreciation.

Without the support of my friends, I would not have had the emotional energy needed to press onward through the inevitable challenges of writing a book. Pam, Miriam, Diana, Cindy, Patricia, and Freddy, thank you all so very, very much! Your sincere enthusiasm and grasp of what I'm trying to say in my books gives me the courage to overcome my doubts and keep writing. Thanks!

Special thanks must also go to my young editor-friends, Zach and Anna — your observations were most helpful. And Mark, thank you for reading and re-reading my manuscript.

Thanks also to the members of my book club for their interest in my writing efforts, especially Lynn, who throws a heck of a great book-signing party!

All my family, near and far, helped by cheering me on. Nina and Lucille, Maryanne too, thank you so much for your enthusiasm. Johnny and Barbara, thank you for sharing my excitement — you encouraged me enormously.

Finally, an especially heart-felt thanks to Devon and Cory — you are my inspiration. And to Ron, how can I ever thank you enough? I could never have done it without you, Honey.

Introduction

Wishing on the Midnight Star is a story about two brothers, one of whom has Asperger's Syndrome, a condition on the autism spectrum. My two sons, Devon and Cory, inspired me with their wonderfully loving and sometimes raging relationship. (Although they were my inspiration, it should be noted that this book is a work of fiction.) Since I wrote my first book, *Buster and the Amazing Daisy*, for Devon, I felt it was only fair to write a book for Cory also. So *Wishing on the Midnight Star* is for Cory and is told from an Aspie sibling's point of view.

Chapter 1

Wishing on the Midnight Star

Rattle, bang! Rattle bang! Rattle, bang-bang!

"Would you quit that!" I poked my brother. "I can't even hear the TV!"

Rattle, bang! Nic kept jiggling and kicking at our bed railing. Besides, the top bunk is mine.

"Get off my bed!" I nudged him with my elbow.

He kept kicking.

"You're bonkers," I told him as I started down the ladder. I planned to turn up the volume on the TV.

Then, wham! His foot smacked into my chin and launched me into space. I snatched at the air, flapping my arms and trying to fly. This didn't work. Obviously. I headed backwards and down. Everything spun around me in slow-upside-down motion. I noticed the cobwebs in the corners of the ceiling, along with a dusty old paper airplane. Then, I crash-landed with a thump that shook the whole room. My matchbox car collection rattled on its shelf. My teeth clattered in my mouth. The breath all rushed out of me for a second — *Wheeewf!* — and even though I was mad, I couldn't yell at Nic, couldn't do more than squeak at him. Then I was okay. Lucky thing our beanbag chair was sitting in just the right place.

Nic peeked down at me through the railing. He'd finally stopped rattling the rail. "Alex! Are you okay? I didn't mean to do that! I'm sorry!"

I gritted my teeth and pulled myself up. My knees wobbled. "Yeah, you're going to be a lot sorrier, you—"

"Alexander and Dominic! What are you two doing in there?" It was Mom. She rushed into the room. "What happened?"

"Nothing much. Nic almost busted my back, that's all." I rubbed my rear end. It was still kind of throbbing.

"I didn't mean to — honest, Mom!" Nic whined. "Alex just makes me so mad — he kept bugging me!"

"You were on my bed, remember, you birdbrain!" I glared at him.

"Okay, knock it off or the TV goes off." Mom sounded like she meant it.

My dumb brother kept squawking, so I tried to shut him up. That's when Mom marched over to the TV. *Snick!* G'bye, Nickelodeon!

"Dominic, time for chores," Mom said. "Please go give Butter some fresh water. Alex, the chickens are waiting for their dinner."

I gimped across the room while Nic slithered down the ladder with the speed of a sloth.

"Come on, both of you! Go outside for a while." Mom put her hands on our shoulders and steered us down the hall.

I slammed the door as I went outside. It's so unfair. Mom lets Nic get away with everything. I stepped over Butter, our old golden retriever. She didn't wake up. Dopey old dog, she wouldn't open her eyes if a herd of buffalo thundered over her. Our cat, Winks, sat on the porch rail, sneering at me. That cat has a serious attitude problem. I hissed at her. Then I went out front and dumped some chicken scratch on the ground and started tossing down some wrinkly grapes. The chickens scurried around, pecking like crazy.

My brother drives me crazy. I could hear him in the house, still fussing. And he's 14 — a whole year older than I am!

I sat down on a railroad tie and held out a grape to the old brown hen. When she grabbed it, I grabbed her. She squawked and flapped her wings. Her feathers slapped hard against my face, but it didn't hurt. After a moment she calmed down. "That's a good girl," I crooned. She settled into my lap. Her soft feathers smelled like dust and dry grass.

In a few minutes Nic came out on the porch lugging a big jug of water. I watched him wrestle with it, trying to fill the dog's water bowl. He's such a klutz. Still, he's the only brother I've got and it's not his fault he's so... so different. Like the bunk bed thing. I know he really didn't mean to do that.

"Hey, Nic," I called. "Have you seen Fluffy?"

"No," he said.

"Would you help me find her?"

"Sure!" It seemed he'd already forgotten we were mad at each other, so I decided to forget it too.

Fluffy is our little black hen. She's one of my favorite chickens, even if she is really spookish. She is small and round and fat with feathers. It looks as if she's wearing feather dusters around her feet. She's pretty, but not as tame as the other chickens. When we brought her home from the farm, she tried to run away into the woods. We had to herd her back home.

"C'mon! Let's look up there in the meadow," I said to Nic. "Maybe she's searching for bugs around those rotting logs at the edge of the woods."

"But, it's getting kinda dark."

"Well, duh! That's why we have to go find her." I climbed up the bank and wiggled through the fence. "Fluffy! Here, chickie!" We waded through some tall grass. The swishing sound we made was the only noise out there except for the crickets. There must have been a million of them cranking up their night song. And then a bullfrog down at the pond chimed in. *Bawhoom, bawhoom!* I liked the sound of him.

"Fluffy! Here, chickie!" I called again. The shadows under the fir trees darkened. She could be hiding there and we'd never see her. I shaded my eyes against the glare of the setting sun and stood still, looking in all directions. She wasn't near the fallen logs. She wasn't wandering around the meadow.

I spotted my brother trying to lift a big sunken rock. "I don't think she's under that rock, Nic."

"I know." He laughed and kept lifting. Finally, he tumbled it over. "But something else might be. You never know!"

Big help he was! I walked deeper into the woods. My feet sank down in the deep layer of moldering leaves. Something rustled in the brambles. "Fluffy?"

A little brown bird burst out with a loud tweet. I didn't see Fluffy, so I walked back toward the meadow. Now my brilliant brother was lying in the grass, looking up at the sky.

"You're going to get ticks all over you," I said.

He scrambled to his feet. He loves every kind of bug. Except for ticks. Then he said "I was just trying to figure out what that blob is."

"What blob?"

He pointed to a large Douglas fir. It was uphill from us, and the sunset was right behind it, making the tree look like a huge shaggy black thing.

"See? Over there. The branches are all thin and pointy, but there's that round blob there."

I looked. "Oh, yeah. I see it." I grinned at him and gave him a shove. "That round blob is what we've been looking for."

"I knew that!" Nic chortled. He grabbed me and gave me a noogie, rubbing my scalp with his bony knuckles hard enough to make it tingle.

"Hey! Enough already!" I pulled away and we headed into the woods, keeping an eye on the tree that Fluffy was perched in. The last of the sunlight made her shiny black feathers shimmer with green rainbows.

"Silly bird!" I said when we reached the tree. "Why do you want to stay up there when you've got a nice cozy coop to sleep in?"

Fluffy eyed us and clucked nervously.

"We've got to get her down," Nic said. "Owls and raccoons love chicken suppers." After a moment he added "It's getting dark."

"I know, I know. Just let me think." I looked at the tree trunk. The lower branches were cut off. A ways up, there was a nice bunch of branches growing up the trunk, almost like a ladder. If I could just reach them, it'd be easy. Fluffy really wasn't up very high.

I looked at Nic. "Kneel down."

"What?"

"I said, kneel down — you know, make like a bench."

"Okay." Nic leaned over and planted his hands in the dirt. His head hung down and his rear end poked up.

"Nic, I said a bench, not a skateboard ramp." I pushed his back and shoulders into a level position and stepped aboard.

"Owwww! Hurry up!" Nic gasped, his back shaking.

I grabbed the branch above me and hauled myself up. Then I started climbing. Fluffy flapped her wings. "Don't you go anywhere, you silly chicken." I was right below her on a good solid branch. As I reached for her, she edged away. Following her, I sidestepped along the bigger branch and hung on to the smaller ones. I was

kind of like a scaredy-cat tightrope walker. One tumble a
day is plenty.

"She's trying to get away," my brother told me.

"I can see that."

"Well, why don't you grab her?"

I looked down at him. I felt like spitting. "What do
you think I'm trying to do?"

Fluffy made her angry crocodile growling noise and
shifted her feet.

"C'mon, Fluffy," I coaxed. "Good chickie-chickie-
chickie." I could tell she was thinking about jumping.
"Don't do it, Fluffy — you'll be sorry!"

I looked at all those spiky twigs. She could get hurt
bashing through them. So could I. I really hated heights.
I wanted to get this over with. I pulled at the limb she was
perched on and stretched myself up on my toes. "Got
you!" I snagged her, holding her feet snugly.

She screeched and pecked and jerked herself around
like I was some kind of chicken-eating monster.

I hung tight. Pulling her over to me, I tucked her
under my arm and started down. It was a bit tricky
climbing down a tree like that, one-handed. But I was
fine until this dumb mosquito started pestering my ear.
This distracted me. And then Nic started yapping about
something. A small shadowy body zipped by my face. A
bat. I knew it wasn't like a vampire or anything, but I
didn't like it buzzing so close. I lost my concentration
and then my balance.

For a few seconds I slammed down through the branches. They scratched and banged me, but when I hit the ground I was still holding Fluffy.

"Hey!" Nic yelled. "Watch where you're landing!"

I stood up slowly, trying to ease the ache out of my hip.

I guess we were making some noise because just then Mom started hollering for us. "Come in, come in, wherever you are!" I could see her way down the hill. She stood on the back porch with the kitchen light glowing behind her.

"Coming!" we yelled. Pushing through the bushes, we headed for home. As I tossed Fluffy into the chicken house, I heard a great horned owl. *Who-whooo! Who-whooo!* He always sounded kind of lonely to me. Hungry, too.

"I'm glad we found Fluffy," Nic said.

"Me too."

As I limped toward the house, Nic clutched my arm. "I really didn't mean to push you off the bunk, you know."

"I know."

"You could've broken your neck. Or suffered some other serious injury."

"I know, but I didn't. I'm fine."

"You're not fine — I can see your leg hurts." Nic's fingers tightened.

"Really, Nic. I'm okay."

"Not okay! I saw you limping! You shouldn't lie, Alex."

"All right. I'm a little sore," I muttered as I shook loose from him. "But it's mostly from falling out of that tree. Which wasn't your fault, correct?"

"Correct." Nic huffed. "Why didn't you say so?"

I clamped my lips together and hurried down the hall to wash up for dinner. My brother has this thing about the truth. I mean, the absolute, down-to-the-last-teensy-detail truth.

We had pork chops and baked potatoes for dinner. The chops were dried out, like always, but I knew Mom's berry pie would even things out. I had snitched a sneak pre-taste earlier. It was awesome. My mouth watered for more, but when Nic pulled the foil off the pie, he noticed the empty space.

"Alex! You spoiled the pie!"

"I didn't spoil it — I just—"

"You just squished it all up — look at that messy purple ooze. Besides, you're supposed to eat your dinner first," Nic bossed. "Mom, look what Alex did." He pointed at the pie.

Mom's mouth tightened into an annoyed line.

"Oh, don't be dopey, you little doofus! It doesn't matter."

"Don't call me dopey doofus, you moron! Mom, Alex is being rude."

Mom started to say something, but I didn't wait to hear it. She always defended Nic.

I shoved back from the table, making a loud screech with my chair, and stomped off to my room. I kicked the door shut with a bang. There was nothing on TV.

19

I wasn't in the mood for homework — was I ever? It was so hot and stuffy in our room, getting to sleep was a joke.

After a few hours, I heard my grandpa's old clock strike midnight. Maybe some fresh air would help. I eased off the bunk and got a drink of water out in the kitchen. And helped myself to a piece of that pie. It tasted perfect, now that I could eat it in peace. As I forked it down, I wandered out to the deck where it was cool.

The sky reminded me of a bedspread I used to lie on when I napped at my grandmother's house, a thick, dark velvet bedspread. This was many years ago, of course. Anyway, one day Grandma left her little manicure scissors out on the nightstand and I cut about a hundred tiny holes in that beautiful cloth. When I held it up to the lamp, the light shone through all those tiny cut-outs like glittering stars. It looked real pretty — just like the sky tonight.

I leaned against the rail and scanned the sky. I found the Big Dipper, and then I looked at the brightest star. My mom always used to bring me out when I was little and recite that poem for me. "Star light, star bright, first star I see tonight, I wish I may I wish I might, have the wish I wish tonight." I liked to wish on the brightest star. At midnight, the brightest star had some special magic in it, I used to tell myself. Tonight I just stared at that midnight star and wished... I didn't know exactly what I was wishing for. Just that things would be different. And the next day they were.

Chapter 2

School Day Blues

It started out like any other day. My brother refused to wake up, then put on a soiled shirt and got all grumbly mad because Mom made him change into a fresh one. It's the same old thing every morning. Then Nic didn't want to take his medicine. "I don't need it, Mom! My brain is just fine," he argued. "I'm in eighth grade, why do you treat me like a baby?"

Nic doesn't always act like an eigth-grader. He has autism, something he was born with. It makes his brain work differently than the rest of us. Some people with autism can't even talk or take care of themselves at all. But Nic is part of a group that has a kind of mild autism called Asperger's Syndrome. Aspies can talk all right and sometimes they're very smart in certain ways. Like Nic. He's great at reading and vocabulary and history facts, like who, what, and when. But this morning he was having one of his dumb temper tantrums.

"We're going to be late for school," Mom said, kind of grumpy-like as she hustled us into the car. "C'mon, you guys. I've got to get to work."

Our dining room table is Mom's office, where she does accounting work. She says it's beastly boring, but it pays the bills. Mom wanted to be a doctor, but after one year in med school, her plans got interrupted. Dad had his accident and Nic's condition started needing lots of attention. So, she does taxes and stuff for other people. Also, she's a midwife. She drives all over the mountains helping ladies have their babies.

Mom takes us to school in the mornings because the bus comes way too early, like before our rooster even starts his sunrise screams. In the afternoons we ride the bus home.

This morning Mom kept looking at her watch as we stood in line waiting for our late slips. Usually, Nic's aide was there, ready to help him through his day. But, this morning his aide was late. So Mom had to wait with Nic and see that he got to class okay.

Standing in line with Nic is torture. If he's in a bad mood like today, he makes a fuss and everyone stares at us. If he's in a good mood, they still stare because Nic will be jiggling and hopping around like a wind-up toy that someone wound too tight. He can't just stand there like everyone else. Not Nic.

Usually, I stand in a different part of the line and don't look at him. Not everybody knows he's my brother.

That morning, I decided to take a chance and make a run for my classroom. I slid into the seat just a few minutes after the second bell rang. Ms. Cortley looked at me and raised her eyebrows. But she didn't send me back for a late slip. She's pretty cool, actually the nicest of the seventh-grade teachers.

We did some work and I was so bored I almost fell asleep. Then we had a math test. I think I only got maybe two or three answers right. I hate numbers; they don't make any sense. Yep, the whole dumb day was going along like always.

At recess I was playing three-flies-up with some other guys. Next to us some kids were playing dodge ball. All at once, this horrible screaming cut through the air. It was my brother, of course. He must have wandered by the dodge ball game and gotten bashed. He was thrashing around on the ground, yelling his head off. Where was his aide? Someone was supposed to be watching him. Finally, the aide came hurrying over with her coffee sloshing out of its cup.

I slunk away. Recess was almost over anyway.

The rest of the day was okay until the last recess. I was running past the boy's bathroom when I heard a familiar sound — my brother screeching. Again.

"What's the matter now?" I asked as I walked in. But then I saw Todd Hammerton, one of the school's worst bullies. Lots of kids call him Todd the Toad, but not to his face. He's all high on himself because he's big and strong, a total jock. He lives in a really cool house with a giant swimming pool and everything like that. But, I know he's got a real streak of poison inside. I hate the way he's so mean. He always kisses up to adults in a really smarmy, totally disgusting way. The worst part is that some dopey grown-ups actually fall for it.

Anyway, Todd had Nic backed into a corner and was snarling in his face. "C'mon, you little dummy! Hand it over. I know you've got a chocolate bar in your pocket."

Nic huddled against the wall, eyes scrunched tight. "Leave me alone!" he yelled.

"C'mon!" Todd poked him in the shoulder. Hard.

"Hey! Bug off, creep!" I can't stand bullies, especially when they pick on Nic.

Todd straightened up and turned to face me. "Mind your own business, dog doo!" His pale blue eyes looked like dead fish eyes.

"Alex!" Nic ran over and hugged me.

I pushed him away. "Get off!"

"Ahhh, ain't that sweet!" Todd sneered. "Little squirrelly Dominic has a bodyguard! Ain't that sweet!" He stuck his hands in his pockets and swaggered out like he'd successfully finished some important business. I wanted to finish him!

"Alex, you saved my life! How can I ever repay you?" Nic grabbed my hand.

Oh, puleeezzz! Nic watches too many dopey movies. I just jerked away and headed out the door.

"Alex, here, you can have my Snickers bar!" Nic followed me, plucking at my arm. His fingers always feel sticky.

"That's okay. I'm not hungry, Nic. See you later!" I sprinted to the far side of the playground and started punching the tetherball really hard. I hate recess.

So, the day was rolling along in its usual miserable way, when we got on the bus to go home. Nic sat up front next to the driver. I walked back to my usual place at the rear. The middle of the bus filled up with the rest of the kids on our route, including good old Todd the Toad.

Then, someone new climbed on board. It was Brianna Santos. She'd never ridden our bus before. Brianna is short and tiny all over, but you can always spot her. She has these brilliant white teeth and when she smiles her whole face seems to light up. She's energetic and bouncy and the way she laughs — it's like little silver bells.

She was standing at the front of the aisle, gazing down the rows of seats. A few kids slid over to make room for her.

I looked away before she could see me staring at her. Then I heard a voice I knew too well.

"Brianna," the voice chirped. "Do you want to sit with me? I'll tell you about my chickens."

When I looked back, I couldn't believe my eyes. Brianna Santos was sitting down, way up front, right next to Nic. I could hear him babbling away, talking her tiny ears off. For once I wished I was sitting close to my brother. But my luck was about to take a dive.

For the rest of the way home I watched Nic and Brianna. Whenever she turned her head to talk to Nic, I'd admire her nose — it tilts up just a tiny bit, real cute.

Once, as she reached up and tucked her hair behind her ear, she glanced back at me. I made sure I wasn't looking at her at that moment.

When we reached our bus stop, not too many kids were left on the bus, but Brianna still sat there. I stood up. I'm cool, I told myself. I'm very cool. I slung my backpack over my shoulder and strode toward the front of the bus. Slow and easy, shoulders back, eyes straight ahead. I was walking towards Brianna Santos.

I was trying to think of something to say and that's why I forgot to watch out for things in my way. Things like Todd's foot which shot out and tripped me, making me crash to the floor and spill everything out of my unzipped backpack. Making me look like a total fool. I was too embarrassed to say a word as I shoved all my books and stuff back into the pack. But I gave Todd a look that let him know I was not going to forget this.

I leaped out of the bus. My face felt like I had a really bad sunburn. I was so humiliated I almost didn't hear her.

Someone was calling "Hey, you dropped your key chain!"

I turned around. It was Brianna Santos, dangling my key chain and smiling at me. I stood there like a dummy. I couldn't think.

She jogged up the slope with dainty little steps. "Here!" As she dropped the key chain into my hand, her fingers touched mine.

I fumbled with the key chain, and dropped it. As I picked it up, all my stuff dumped out. Again!

There was that silvery giggle. "You're Alex, right? Nic's brother? You look kind of like him."

Glancing up the street at Nic, I nodded. "Uhuh."

"He sure knows a lot about animals," she said.

"Uhuh."

"Well, the bus is waiting."

"Uhuh."

She stood looking at me for another second, her eyebrows quirked into a question. Like Hellllo? Can you talk? Then, smiling that stop-your-heart smile, she said "See you later."

I tried to think of what to say. Words swarmed through my mind like a bunch of buzzing bees. Finally, I thought of something. "Yeah," I said, bobbing my head up and down like a yo-yo. Brilliant, Alex. Could I possibly be less impressive? Yes.

Chapter 3

Magic and Mud

When I looked up, the bus was gone. So was she. I stood in the street. What had just happened here? True, I hadn't made such a great impression. But still, things weren't totally bleak. Brianna Santos knew my name. She wanted to see me again. She said so herself. Suddenly, the sky seemed bluer and the air smelled sweeter.

Nic, bending with the weight of his overstuffed backpack, shuffled across the street to the frog pond. I followed him. We circled the pond and spotted one really big bullfrog. We tried to catch him, but he was way too fast. Then Nic messed around in the mud for a while. Nic says squeezing mud feels real nice to him.

Actually, our mud is good adobe — you can even make pottery with it. So.

Nic sees and hears and smells in a special way, too. Certain sights, like sparkly, spinning things, he really loves. If he hears certain sounds, like thundering fireworks, he freaks.

We hung around the pond for a while. I wandered along the water's edge and checked out the tracks in the damp soil. Lots of deer; their v-shaped prints are easy to recognize. Then I spotted little hand-like prints. Raccoon. It must have come down to hunt frogs. A few tiny forked tracks. Probably quail. That was about it.

Finally, I said "Almost time to go home."

For once, Nic didn't argue. After a minute, we trudged up the hill.

"Brianna and her mom just moved into a new house right down the road from us," Nic told me. "The old Billoughby place. That's why Brianna's riding our bus now."

"Hmmm." I didn't want to seem too eager for details, even with Nic. No worries; Nic was in one of his chattery moods all of a sudden.

"She wants to come over some time, see our chickens and stuff," he continued, but I wasn't really listening.

Brianna Santos being our neighbor seemed a more interesting idea to concentrate on. Finally, I noticed Nic was looking pretty wound up. He had this big goofy grin on his face and his fingers flickered with excitement.

He whispered something to me.

"Nic, you don't need to whisper. No one's around."

"But it's a secret. You have to whisper if it's a secret," he explained.

"Okay. Whatever."

"I think Brianna's in love with me. She told Lottie Whitmore that she thinks I'm cute." Nic leaned really close to my face. He smelled like pond muck.

I stopped walking and stared at him, at his pointy chin and elf ears. If you ignored the mud spattered over his coppery freckles and maybe smoothed down Nic's rumpled hair, he might look okay. But cute? I don't know. It's not the kind of thing that guys usually notice about their brothers.

"Did you hear me, Alex?" Nic asked, impatient.

"I hate to burst your bubble, Nic, but that's a crazy idea. Why would a girl like Brianna Santos..." My voice trailed off as I looked into Nic's round, rip-roaring, fire-blue eyes. They almost glowed. I turned away. Maybe I was wrong. Either way, I couldn't blow that happy blaze out. "I mean, what I mean is... you just met her today."

"Haven't you ever heard of love at first sight?"

I didn't answer. I just shrugged and walked into our house. You can never win an argument with Nic. Besides, maybe there is such a thing as love at first sight.

Nic followed me, wanting to continue the conversation, but Mom headed him off with milk and cookies.

"Hi, guys, here's your snack. Nic, you need to wash up quick. You can eat while we drive to your ST group."

ST stands for Social Therapy. Nic goes once a week to learn how to understand people and get along easier. I hope it works.

The next afternoon I got on the bus and walked to the rear. Todd was too busy impressing a couple of girls to hassle me today. I couldn't believe how they thought he was so cool. Okay, so he's tall and plays basketball and he's got this smooth tanned skin. Not one pimple. And he never has a bad hair day. Thinking about hair, I whipped out my baseball cap and jammed it over my head. Ms. Cortley won't let us wear hats in class, but she doesn't rule this bus.

Nic settled into his seat up front. He fidgeted and craned his neck to see who was climbing aboard. The doors swung shut with a loud hiss, and the bus lurched forward. Nic leaped to his feet. "Wait! Brianna's not here yet! Brianna Santos rides this bus. Don't you remember?" he shouted at our bus driver. "You can't leave without Brianna!"

"Take it easy, Dominic," Mrs. Guttman said. "I'm sure Brianna will be back Monday. She went home with a friend today, okay?"

"Uh, uh! Not okay," Nic muttered. His fists clenched, unclenched. Again and again.

C'mon, Nic. Don't lose it! I watched, holding my breath. Then, grumbling, Nic pulled out a book and stuck his face right up close to the pages.

Now he was quiet. I slumped back in the seat. Thank goodness it was Friday.

Nic is a big-time bookworm. He gets hooked on a certain subject and that's all he reads until he's worn out the pages on almost every single book ever written about it. And he remembers every word, it seems. His mind snaps down on facts like a Macabee rat-trap. His current special interest is true-crime books. Geez! He can toss around police slang like a sergeant.

When we got to our stop, Nic and I got off and started hiking up the hill. He puffed and panted, carrying practically a whole library of books in his pack. After a minute, he paused. "Brianna wasn't on the bus today," he told me.

Jeez! Like this was news! But just to be agreeable, I said "Yeah, I know."

"She'll be back on Monday," Nic said.

"Yeah, probably so."

"No! Not probably! She will be!" Nic corrected me loudly. "Mrs. Guttman said she was sure."

"Okay, whatever," I muttered. I hate it when he gets like this.

"Don't you 'whatever' me!" Nic snapped. "You need to keep the facts straight."

"Would you just chill, Nic?"

"I'll chill when I'm good and ready!" He stumbled and fell to his hands and knees. His pack slipped up and settled on his head like a lumpy overstuffed turban. "Agghhh! Look what you made me do!"

As if it's my fault! I ran for home, ran far enough ahead of my brother so I didn't have to hear him hollering. As I got near our house, I took a short-cut through the orchard. Our big rooster flapped his wings and crowed. He and the hens were out under the old apple trees, scratching around for bugs.

The rooster was feeling mean today. We didn't call him the Beast for nothing. He crab-walked over to me, stomping sideways and crowing loudly. He lowered his head like a snake ready to strike and fluffed up his neck feathers, trying to be a cobra. I kicked at him. I was feeling mean today too.

That night I couldn't sleep. I couldn't even breathe in that room after my row with my brother. So I did what I always do. Outside on the deck the air swelled with the scent of sweet hay and pine trees. The stars glittered like ice chips. It's so dumb, wishing on a star. I used to say that poem every night, wishing that my brother would be cured of his autism. But he never will be.

Even though I've known Nic all my life, sometimes I feel like I don't really know him at all. His mind goes places I can't follow. And I don't really want to go there. Sometimes those places don't seem good to me. I used to worry that I'd catch the autism, but Mom's told me a million times that it's not contagious. I know I'll never catch it, but I sure wish I could cure it.

After a while I heard the coyotes yipping down in the gully below our house. I hate them. We used to have a cat, a beautiful big cozy cat. His name was Cheyenne and he'd curl up with me in bed and purr really loud. He helped me go to sleep. But one night, when he was out hunting, I heard a scream so awful it froze my insides. I knew it was him. I ran outside and called and called him, but then it got quiet except for something rattling and snapping in the brush. Coyotes. Anyway, I never saw Cheyenne again. Only a few tufts of his fur. I threw up when I saw the blood on them.

I know coyotes don't attack people. Hardly ever, anyway. A little kid got dragged off in the hills a few miles north of here. That was a few years ago, during a drought when all the wildlife was stressed. That was a very rare thing. It hardly ever happens. Suddenly shivering, I hurried back to bed.

The next morning Mom woke me up early. "Mrs. Young's baby is coming. I don't think it'll take too long, but you never know."

Mom was smiling away, all chirpy and cheery, even though it was still kind of dark out. She sure loves bringing out those babies even if it's in the middle of the night, which it lots of times is.

Actually, my mom is almost always in a good mood; she's kind of goofy, too. Nic says she's "pathologically cheerful." I wouldn't mind her being happy and all, but she's noisy about it. Always humming or, worse, singing. She belts out these songs from old movies, but she changes the words around. And her voice wobbles way off key. It's irritating.

As she smoothed my hair out of my face, Mom said "Karen will be here in a while."

I groaned.

"Oh, she's not so bad. Maybe you can talk her into making blueberry pancakes."

"I don't feel like pancakes. I just want cereal." Actually, the pancakes sounded wonderful, but I didn't want to give Mom any encouragement on the whole babysitter thing. It was humiliating, really. I am thirteen years old. And Nic was well… fourteen. Sort of. I guess Karen is okay. She tells Nic stories and listens to him blab about whatever his latest interest is. And she does make good pancakes. It's only when she tries to boss me that I can't stand her.

Mom patted my cheek. "All right then." She leaned down over the lower bunk, and I heard her murmur something to Nic, who was wrapped in his blanket like a mummy. He was still asleep. A moment later she stepped up on the bunk ladder. "Have a good day. I'll be back later."

As she planted a kiss on my forehead, I breathed in the smell of lemon soap. It woke me up some more, and I decided to get up. Anyway, the Beast was crowing like crazy and I knew I wouldn't be getting back to sleep.

I caught a snatch of Mom's singing as she headed to the car. "Raindrops on roses, and bald-headed babies," she warbled. Ughh! I walked out to the kitchen to have some orange juice and think about what I wanted to do today. I couldn't think of anything much. Maybe I'd see if Jimmy or one of the Castro brothers wanted to bike ride down to the lake. But I'd have to wait to call them. Nobody's awake yet. Just me.

The rooster was still making a racket and the hens were all muttering, probably wishing they were out of the coop and away from him. I stuck on my sandals and went out. Dawn was my favorite time of day. Sunbeams squinted through the pine trees. It was peaceful. The blue jays were starting to squawk as they squabbled over the birdseed on the porch railing. One had a topknot of feathers sticking up, mohawk-style. The feathers bounced as he pecked. Up near the chicken coop I could hear some doves cooing. They were probably gobbling up some of yesterday's chicken scratch. Maybe I'd go let the chickens out now. They liked to get out and about while it was still cool.

I started up the pathway, then I remembered that the Beast was getting meaner every day and I didn't even have my boots on. I grabbed the rooster stick.

There he was, a big guy with a scarlet comb and a cocky gleam in his yellow eyes. He stretched out his wings and beat his feathers like he thought he was Tarzan, king of the chicken coop. He looked up at the sky and told the sun to hurry it up. Then he crowed, but it didn't sound like cocka-doodle-doo. It sounded like someone screaming and gargling at the same time. He made this noise about twelve times then he looked around as if he was waiting for applause. The hens ignored him.

"Hey, chickie-chick-chicks!" I greeted them. The hens clustered around the gate, clucking. When I opened it, some of them rushed out, some of them strutted out slowly. All except Fluffy. She always scuttles into the nesting shed and hides until no one is around. She'd sneak out later.

I kept an eye on the rooster and he kept his eye on me. As he crab-stepped past, he stabbed his claws into the ground, making little puffs of dust shoot up. I stomped back at him with the rooster stick.

A year ago we got a few young chickens from the feed store. They were supposed to be hens, but after a while, one started looking different from the others. Her neck and tail were longer and she had a bunched-up floppy red comb. She turned into a rooster. The only good thing about the rooster was that someday we'd have baby chicks popping out all over the place. I could hardly wait.

I was starting to get hungry so I headed back to the kitchen. There was a note on the counter. It was for Nic, but I read it anyway. Mom was reminding him to take his medicine. Fat chance! He'd forget two seconds after he saw the note and then we'd have a rotten day. I snatched his sports bottle out of the fridge and shook it up real good. Nic hates lumps.

When I walked in to our bedroom, Nic snapped shut his leather-backed notebook. He was always scribbling away in that beat-up old thing. "Here, Nic." I held out the sports bottle.

Without a word, he grabbed it and started chugging. He finished in a flash. "Thanks, Alex." He handed back the bottle and let loose a loud chittering burrrrrp.

Well, at least he was mellow. At the moment, anyway. The day was going pretty well, I thought. But things can change fast.

My stomach rumbled. Maybe some corn flakes would hold me until Karen got here and made pancakes. I wondered if it was too early to call anyone. I dialed the Castro brother's number and got a busy signal. Then, I remembered. They had a sixteen-year-old sister. I gave up on them right away. Next I tried Jimmy. His mom answered and said he was out playing catch with his brother. He'd call me back later. I thought about calling Jeremy Fisher, but he usually ended up teasing Nic. I wasn't that desperate.

I dumped some cereal into the bowl and wandered around, thinking. I passed the mirror in the living room and stopped to check myself out. Not a single pimple, but my old Batman costume was definitely dorky. I only wore it for summer pajamas when everything else was in the laundry basket or dumped on the floor somewhere. Who cared what it looked like? This morning my hair stuck out all over in stiff snarls. I pulled the black masked hood over it. Oh, yeah, now I'm just awesome. Yeah, right! I flashed my yellow fangs, then turned away in disgust.

As I shoveled in the last spoonful and tipped the bowl back for a good slurp of cereal-sweet milk, I heard a knock on the front door.

Chapter 4

Horror in the Morning

Funny, I wasn't expecting anyone except Karen. And she doesn't knock. But, like a dope, I walked over and peeked out the living room window. What I saw startled me so much I jerked backwards, which caused the last bit of milk to splash over my face and up my nose. I snorted and choked.

"Hello?" the visitor called.

I tried to swallow a cough, but it came out anyway. I sounded like a hippo strangling.

Brianna Santos was standing outside my front door. I couldn't believe it. So, like a total idiot, I craned my neck around and peeked out again. To make sure. Oh, my gosh. It was her. What to do? What to do? What to do? My thoughts scurried around like mice in a maze.

I couldn't tear myself away from the sight of Brianna Santos standing there at my doorstep with the morning sunlight dancing on her hair and her long lashes casting shadows on her cheeks and that tiny secret smile dimpling so that anyone with eyes would be totally bewitched. Oh, my gosh!

And, then, in a truly terrible slow-motion kind of way, her eyes began to shift up toward my foolish face and the sweet look on her face twisted into something like... like... I don't know, as if maybe she'd spotted the cat barfing up mouse guts. Her eyes narrowed and her nose wrinkled up. Maybe she just didn't recognize me with milk dribbling all down my face. Also there was the bat mask.

Anyway, the spell was broken. I leaped into action. With a speedy spin, I slammed my back up against the wall. Panting, I tried to think. She'd seen me or seen something. Definitely. She knew someone was here. Did she recognize me with cereal on my face and in a Batman outfit? What to do? What to do? I swiped the milk and a corn flake off my mouth and yanked off the mask. I licked my hands so I could flatten down my hair a little. Then, boldly, I made my move.

I ran as fast as I could across the living room, down the hall, and slid around the corner into my room, slamming the door behind me. Then I locked it, just in case.

Nic blinked at me, sleepy-eyed. "What?" he asked, rubbing his face.

Panting, I stared at him. Finally, I found my breath. "It's Brianna Santos," I gasped. "She's here."

"Where?" he said loudly, looking around the room as if she'd come in with me.

"Shhhhh." I squeezed my eyes shut, trying to concentrate.

"Oh, yeah," my brother said, yawning so wide his jaw clicked.

"Oh, yeah? What do you mean, oh, yeah?" I opened my eyes and looked at him.

"I asked her to come over today. What time is it? Is she still there?" He slung the blanket onto the floor and headed for the door. He was wearing his underpants. Just his underpants.

"Nic, wait!" I grabbed his shoulder. "You can't go out like that!"

He stopped. "Oh. You're right."

I could hear knocking at the door. We both yanked on jeans and T-shirts and I rammed my cap over my head. "Hey, Nic?" I said.

"Yeah?"

"Next time will you tell me if you're expecting company?"

"Sure." He headed out the door. I headed out the window.

I circled the house, planning my get-away. It was one of those times that I really needed some peace and quiet just by myself. The lake. That'd be just the place. I didn't know how wrong I would be.

I needed to get away from here. Away from Nic, the most irritating brother in all the world. Away from Brianna, the most incredible girl in all the world. Away from the scene of my humiliation. I had to be the biggest fool in all the world.

I jumped on my bike and started pedaling up the driveway, weaving around the potholes. I waved to the babysitter as she pulled in, but ignored her shouts. A second later I fired my bike over a bank, catching some air, and began barreling down the hill towards the lake.

It takes concentration to handle that twisty dirt path, and I didn't have much at that moment. I hit the first dirt bowl wrong and almost collided with a boulder. Then I sideswiped a toyon bush, coming out with red berries stuck in my hair. It took some sharp twigs slashing at my face to get my attention enough so that I slowed down.

After about a mile the path leveled out and a tall metal fence with a padlocked gate barred the way. On the gate a metal sign was painted over with red graffiti. The sign tried to tell you the place belonged to the water district and you shouldn't trespass. The graffiti said something rude. The water folks didn't want kids sneaking in and messing things up. But the sign wasn't meant for someone like me. I'd been coming here for years, and I never left a trace behind. No one ever bothered me. Of course, I usually stayed out of sight. The oak and madrona trees gave plenty of hiding places and if someone did come after me, I could easily discourage them by popping into a patch of poison oak.

I pitched my bike into some bushes and scaled the gate, using the attached sign as a foothold.

Hiking through a grove of eucalyptus trees, I breathed in the familiar spicy smell. It helped calm me. Huge strips of bark and dry leaves littered the ground. I crunched through them, not even spotting the snake until I almost stepped on it. It hissed and rattled its tail, making a menacing buzz in the leaves.

I froze, one foot in the air. I studied the long brown patterned body, my eyes following the twisted loops until I found its tail. I let out my breath and put my foot down. No rattle. It was just a big fat gopher snake.

I bent over him. "You had me fooled for a second, fella. You could give someone a heart attack doing that." As I reached out to stroke him, he slithered away. For a second, my finger trailed over his skin. His scales made smooth little bumps and felt cool. I needed to cool down some more myself.

I walked on and came to the edge of the woods. The lake lay like a huge flat dish made of cobalt blue crystal, not a ripple on it. Near the shore, the hills and trees cast their glassy, upside-down reflections. It was pretty, but I was in an ugly mood.

Standing at the water's edge, I hurled a rock. It skipped and sunk with an angry kerplunk. Then another rock. Two skips. Whoopee-doo. I thought of Brianna. Somehow, someway, I thought maybe she and I could be... friends or... Yeah, right. Dream on, Alex!

I kicked at some rocks. Then I spotted a perfect stone, smooth, round, and flat. I slung it hard. There. It skittered across the water, maybe five, six times.

Restless, I gazed around the lake. No one was here but me. Sometimes rowdies came and partied, but that was usually at night. I was glad to have the place to myself right then. I sat in the shade and pulled off my sandals, shirt, and jeans. My baseball cap, I carefully put on a boulder. It was the last thing my dad gave me, and I take good care of it.

I picked my way down the sandy bank, careful not to step on anything sharp. The soil felt gritty and spongy, nice under my bare feet. As I waded in, the cold water sent shivers all over me. I bent down and splashed my face, then ducked my whole self in. Just for a moment. Gasping with the cold, I shot back up. I jumped and slapped at the water, splashing sparkling droplets high. "Ooooowheeeee!" I hooted.

Diving down, I swam along under the surface. Above me, the water glowed see-through green. The sunlight sent gold streamers shimmering down to the darkness below. It looked like stained glass. I frog-kicked along, cruising through the watery glade. A school of minnows flashed by, zipping back and forth.

Finally, I could think of Brianna without feeling like screaming. Yeah, I'd looked like a fool, but what else was new? I imagined bringing her here sometime, someday when she'd forgotten about today. I could just see her swimming along with me, her long hair all dark and shiny, water sparkling on her face, a beautiful, brown-eyed mermaid.

After a while the bad thoughts were washed away. Mostly. I climbed out. A plastic six-pack loop, now empty of cans, of course, lay next to the water. I scooped it up. A bird or fish might tangle in it. Sometimes people were so stupid. I tucked the trash in the pocket of my jeans and stretched out in the sun to dry off. The smooth hot boulder felt good against my skin and the brightness of the water made my eyes want to shut, but I kept them at least half-open. No telling what might come along. Or who.

Above me, a red-tail hawk soared, searching for a meal. I was getting hungry myself so I gathered up my clothes and got dressed.

As I reached for my cap, I spotted the family of ducks that lived out here. They'd started out with seven ducklings. Only three were left. Some of the fish out here could swallow up a tiny duckling. And of course there were the raccoons and hawks. And coyotes.

I was watching the third duckling scramble to catch up with his mother when, without warning, a blast of gunfire ripped through the silence. Really loud and really close. I almost jumped out of my skin. The ducks splashed and quacked in terror as the water erupted around them. When the commotion settled, the mother duck paddled in circles, calling. Only one duckling trailed her.

I went nuts. "Stop it!" I screamed. "Don't you dare shoot another, you creep!" I ran back and forth scanning the trees. It was hopeless. The shooter could be anywhere. "Don't you shoot another! Do you hear me?"

The silence mocked me.

Suddenly, another volley of shots rang out. Sparks flew on the rock where I'd parked my cap. I dove behind a big fallen log and huddled there, shaking.

Someone laughed.

I quit shaking and sat up. I'd know that ugly laugh anywhere. Furious, I leaped to my feet and yelled "That's not funny, Todd!"

Silence.

"Yeah, I know who you are, you big coward!" I spun all around, trying to see him. "Yeah, real tough guy! Shooting baby ducks!"

I saw a motion behind a bay tree about thirty yards away. This time, the shots blasted my hat up in the air. I caught it as it fell and sprinted for cover in the trees. Maybe it was time to go home.

Burning and cursing, I hiked back to my bike. As I slapped the dust off my cap, I noticed the spatter of holes in it, pellet gun holes. I hated that guy, really hated him.

Chapter 5

The Real Alex Stone
Steps Forward

Monday morning came. It was worse than usual. Nic hated Mondays and he let the whole world know it. We were sitting in our beat-up old station wagon, waiting for Mom. Nic was driving me crazy bossing and badgering me about every little thing.

"Put your backpack where it belongs!" "Quit tapping your foot!" "Buckle your seat belt!" Yammer, yammer, yammer.

"I'm riding my bike to school," I said as I reached for my backpack. "Tell Mom."

"You're not supposed to ride on that road. It's dangerous," Nic lectured as I scrambled out of the car. "I'll have to tell Mom."

"Fine." I pushed at the car door, but Nic pushed back.

"Wait!" he said. "You can give me a ride."

"Like that's going to make it safer?"

"Yes, I'll watch for reckless drivers!" Nic started to climb out after me.

"No!" I shoved him back in and tried to close the door.

"C'mon, Alex! Give me a ride!" He popped back out of the car like a Jack-in-the-Box. I pushed him down on the seat, pulled myself out, and slammed the door.

"Alex! Did you hear me? I'm ready to ride with you again!"

I leaped onto my bike, my backpack thumping my spine. As I pedaled up the driveway, I heard my brother calling after me. "I promise I'll hold on this time!"

The last time I'd given Nic a ride was about four years ago. He couldn't get the hang of bike-riding by himself. Partly, he was scared of trying something new. And, partly, the fast gliding motion spooked him — he didn't trust the brakes to stop him. But one day he agreed to perch behind me on the bike seat and we were having a great time. Too great. Nic got so thrilled he let go of me and started flapping his hands. Crashhhh! Neither of us felt like doing that again.

Nic likes to flap when he's happy. When I was little, like just a baby, I tried it. I ran around, flapping — but it just made my wrists kind of sore.

I'd just reached the top of our driveway when Mom called "Alex! Come back here!"

Oh, great.

"I'll be fine!" I yelled over my shoulder. "It's good exercise, Mom!"

"Alexander Stone!"

"You're going to be late, Mom!" I waved as I coasted down the hill. Mom was into healthy stuff like eggplant and exercise. And she believes in buses. They're safer, she says. But bicycling was a perfect solution. I didn't have to deal with Nic or face Brianna. Or try to stop myself from smashing Todd's fat face into a pulp. But, as I zipped down the narrow, winding road to school, Brianna, Nic, and Todd were all with me anyway, in my thoughts.

I was so busy thinking, I didn't even notice the truck coming up behind me. Not until it honked and zoomed by me. I could feel the hot rush of wind try to knock my bike over.

I hung on tight to the handle bars. The memory of my dad rushed into my mind and I swallowed hard. It was a logging truck that killed him. Squashed his little pick-up flat. That happened five years ago. I pedaled faster, trying to push the sadness away.

Dad used to roughhouse with Nic and me, throw us high in the air and then toss us down on the bed. He had a big rumbling laugh.

When the wild cherry plums ripened, he'd hoist us up on his shoulders and stroll along under the trees so we could pick the fruit. The tiny plums tasted mildly sweet, like an almost ripe pear. One time I bit into a nice plump one and it was so bitter, it puckered up my tongue. I didn't want to ever eat them again, but Dad told me most were sweet and you could never tell until you took a taste.

It's still hard to believe he's really dead.

I almost hit a pothole; swerved at the last second. Shaking my head, I squinted at the road ahead. Dad was strong. He protected us. But nothing protected him.

Now I was the protector. But I wasn't very good at it. I was just a stupid measly punk. Puny for my age. No good at impressing anyone. Have you ever noticed how the harder you try to impress someone, the bigger fool you make of yourself? That's how it seems to me. Every time I thought of Brianna, I wished I was taller and stronger and smarter and cooler. But every time I was around her, I felt smaller and dumber and dorkier. For example, what happened the next weekend — all I was trying to do was be a hero. Dumb idea. I'm definitely not the heroic type.

It started out such a perfect Saturday morning, a sunny fall day with a cool nip in the air. We'd just finished some scrambled eggs. I had no homework, for once. The day smelled sweet like the Concord grapes that dangled, dark and ripe, on the vines along our porch. Nic slouched out there on the wicker rocking chair, just rocking, munching, and jotting something in his old notebook. He thought he was some kind of naturalist, always writing down his observations. His fingers were turning the pages purple. The grapes smelled so good, I picked some for myself.

Out in the brush a quail called "Ha-HA-huh, ha-HA-huh!" It sounded so cheerful, it was hard not to feel that way too. At that moment I couldn't imagine how awful this beautiful morning would turn out to be.

"No one's coming over today or anything, right, Nic?"

He chewed with juicy gusto and then leaned over the porch railing to spit out the seeds.

"Just Brianna."

"Oh." Just Brianna. I stood up and peered up the driveway, carefully controlling my panic.

"Do you like her?" my brother asked.

Do I *like* her? "No," I answered and it was the truth. I didn't like her — I was crazy about her.

"That's too bad. Because she really likes you," Nic remarked. He popped a few more grapes in his mouth.

"What? What makes you think that? Did she tell you that? What did she say? I thought she had a crush on you." I knew I was babbling, but I couldn't seem to stop.

Nic munched and stared up into the oak tree. "Oh, look at that squirrel! Isn't he cute?"

"Nic! We are talking about Brianna Santos. I thought *you* liked her." I didn't know why I was having this conversation with Nic. What did he know, anyway?

"Well, I do like her. Just as a friend, you know."

I will never understand my brother.

"Why don't you ask Brianna yourself?" Nic said as if anybody could talk to her.

"Me?" Jeez, he gets dumber every moment. I mean, like, what could I say to Brianna Santos? "When's she coming?" I asked.

"About ten."

I hurried into the kitchen and checked the clock on the window sill. It was ten after ten. I splashed some

water on my face and dressed in about thirty seconds. As I stuck my feet into my sandals, I glanced out the window.

Brianna was walking down the driveway. She looked so… so… incredibly wonderful. Be cool, be cool, I told myself.

I rushed over to the front door. My hands were sweaty. I couldn't even turn the doorknob. I raced into the bathroom to wash up again. I checked myself out in the mirror — aghhhh! My lips were purple-black. Those darn grapes. Desperately I scrubbed at them, but the soap made me gag. While I was spitting into the sink, I noticed my tongue. Black, too. I realized I just was not ready for this.

I dashed into the bedroom and flopped down on the lower bunk. I took deep breaths the way Mom showed me to do that time I cut my foot and had to have stitches. It worked then to calm me, but it wasn't working now. My heart was trying to hammer right through my chest. I was hopeless.

In a few minutes I heard Nic and Brianna talking. I peeked through the opening in the curtains. Nic was walking around the yard with Brianna, yakking away. He introduced her to Mom, whose voice was so syrupy sweet it made me want to barf. I know she meant well, but jeez. Finally, Mom quit dripping all over Brianna and got back to washing dishes.

Nic and Brianna headed down to the woodshed. Nic pointed to the roof where a couple of chickens were laying on their sides, wings stretched out, sunbathing.

Brianna thought this was cute. I could hear her silvery giggle. Nic, slow and cautious, crawled up a plank to the shed's roof. Brianna, graceful and sure-footed, spread her arms like a tightrope artist and followed him.

What does Brianna see in my brother, anyway? Nic said... Nic said... What did he say? He just liked her as a friend. Okay, what was the other? That she liked me? No. That she really liked me. Of course, sometimes Nic doesn't exactly understand that kind of stuff. He's probably way off base. Still. I stared at her. How would I ever know?

The chickens squawked a bit and moved over. My brother and this girl I can't take my eyes off of settled down on the roof. Then I did take my eyes off her. Just for a second. I grabbed Nic's binoculars and pressed them to my eyes.

I know. It seems kind of rude. Like spying. Well, okay, it was spying. But I couldn't help myself. I zoomed in on her face. It was even prettier close-up. Her eyes always smiled; they crinkled and turned up at the outer corners. And they're dark as a lake on a star-bright night. The sparkling blackness of them contrasted with her skin, which glowed like honey in the sunlight. I know I sound goofy, but anyone seeing her would understand.

Anyway, they chatted. I watched.

After a while, they decided to get down. Nic started crawling backwards down the plank, but suddenly it slipped and crashed to the ground. He yelped and started to slide off the roof. Brianna grabbed him and managed to pull him back. Now they were peering over the edges of the roof, trying to find a way down.

They were stranded. I couldn't believe my luck! This was my big chance. Brianna and Nic looked up toward the house. I jerked away from the window and quickly put the binoculars back where I found them. I took a deep breath. Now, finally, Brianna Santos could meet the real Alex Stone, smart and cool. The coolest.

Oh, jeez, was I ever wrong.

Chapter 6

Attack of the Monstrous Midgits

As I strapped on my sandals, I heard them start calling my name. I shrugged the tightness out of my shoulders. I strolled down to the woodshed, carefully arranging my face into a calm and noble expression. Alexander the Great to the rescue.

"We need the plank put up," Nic said.

"Sure, okay. No problem."

"Hi, Alex." It was her. Brianna Santos was talking to me. I looked up at her. About a thousand frogs were jumping around in my belly. Errrp! I smiled and tried to think of something smart. Should I say hi or hello?

"Hilo, Bianca." Dang it! What was I saying?

She smiled uncertainly and looked at Nic.

"He means to greet you," Nic explained. She nodded, looking at me with concern.

You are an idiot, I told myself. Just close your mouth and move the stupid plank. I grabbed it and hauled it across the dry grass to a more level area. It bumped over some dirt clods and a splinter stabbed my finger, but I never even winced. I leaned the plank up against the shed's roof and shifted it around so that it didn't tilt sideways. It was almost perfectly level.

All at once the grass around my ankles felt weird. It was moving around my feet, crawling on me. But grass doesn't crawl. And grass doesn't sting. Gasping, I looked down and saw ants. Big red ants. About a zillion of them. They were attacking me. I dropped the plank and started goose-stepping around, jerking my knees up real high and slapping at my legs like mad. The ants swarmed all over my feet, stinging like crazy. It felt like fiery needles stabbing in between my toes. Worse, there was a huge army of the horrid little monsters crawling up my legs. I did a standing broad jump; I must have leaped at least ten feet. But the ants were still on me, marching onward, biting and burning. Frantic, I swatted at my jeans and stomped my feet.

Then, the situation got serious. With a hideous feeling of horror, I realized the ants were inside my jeans and traveling upward. Some were attacking the tender area behind my knees! A few were advancing on the upper parts of my thighs. In another second they'd be biting my... A scream of pure horror burst out of me.

I had to do something!

I couldn't believe it. I was jumping out of my jeans in front of Brianna Santos. She was right there, watching. She saw my underwear. She saw my pathetic, skinny white thighs. This was the worst day of my life.

As I sprinted toward the house, I heard Nic howling with laughter. He is the worst brother anyone could ever have!

Mom must have heard the commotion because, as I bounded up the steps, she flung open the door. I almost knocked her over, trying to get inside.

"Alexander Stone! What—"

"Ants!" I bellowed, dancing around, slapping away the last of the little monsters.

"Oh, honey — you've got bites all over you."

No kidding, Mom.

"Here, come on." She hustled me into the bathroom and ran some cool water into the tub. I stood there, shaking and moaning.

I'll get some oatmeal — that'll help soothe those bites." Mom hurried out of the room.

I wasn't waiting for any cereal. It felt like my legs were on fire. I pulled off my shirt and shoes and hopped into the tub. The cold water made me gasp, but it felt good too.

Mom came in and dumped a bunch of oatmeal into the water. "Stir it up and put the clumps on the ant bites," she said.

I did that and, after a few minutes, that awful stinging started to fade.

"How are you doing, honey?" Mom asked.

I shook my head and shrugged. There were no words for my humiliation. Now that the worst of the pain was over, I had to face the fact that I'd never be able to go near Brianna Santos again. Whenever she saw me, she'd remember how ridiculous I looked jumping around, screaming like a baby. Practically naked. "Mom, I'm okay. Could you leave now? Please?"

"Sure." She gave me a sympathetic smile and walked out, closing the door with a soft click. I climbed out of the tub and locked the door, then plopped back into the water. I laid my head on my knees and squeezed my eyes closed really tight. They leaked anyway.

After a few minutes, I heard voices out in the living room. It was Brianna and that stupid rat fink brother of mine. This was all his fault. He had to have known that ant nest was there. He spends hours studying every last little bug around here. For sure he knew about it! Footsteps clattered down the hallway. One set of steps was light and quick; the other heavier. Brianna and Nic were outside the bathroom door.

I held my breath. Go away! I silently urged.

They continued down the hall. In a moment I heard Nic telling Brianna about his nature collection. I call it his voodoo collection. Over the years he's scouted around the countryside picking up all sorts of strange and disgusting bits of nature — a gopher skull, a raccoon's tail, snake skins, stuff like that. He labeled everything and put it all in a big box. It smelled icky and looked awful.

Yeah, Nic! Way to go! I'm sure Brianna will be fascinated. I hoped she would be grossed out enough to never come over again. I listened.

"Where is that bone from?" she asked. She was being polite.

Nic, the doofus, was babbling on and on about each and every little thing laid out in the whole collection. He was so weird. He was totally obsessed with this stuff. Who cared about a mummified frog?

Oh, wonderful. Now, he'd switched to some gory details of police investigations. His other obsession. Big improvement, Nic!

Then, *thunk! Thunk!*

Darts. Nic was showing off. The only reason he was so good at darts was because he'd been practicing for years, ever since his favorite PE teacher suggested it. Brianna was acting all impressed. What was the big deal about a few bull's eye hits?

After a while I heard the light footsteps again. They passed, heading for the living room.

"Good bye, Mrs. Stone." Brianna walked out the front door and out of my life.

I got out of the tub, wiped the oatmeal goo off, and pulled on my clothes. Nic was still in our room, rattling around with his dumb collection. As I yanked open the bathroom door, he stuck his head around the corner. "Hey, Alex, I'm ready to try bike-riding with you."

I glared at him. My fingers twitched.

"I mean, if you feel like it." He studied my face. "I'm sorry I laughed at you and the ants, but you just looked so — are you okay?" He stopped talking and started backing up, clutching his stupid box. "You look mad."

Duh! I stomped in and snatched the box away from him. I hurled it across the room.

"Alex!" Nic's eyes popped wide open as he yelled. "What's the matter? What're you doing?"

"No, Nic, what were you doing? You made me look like a fool."

"I'm sorry! Sorry, sorry, sorry!" he screeched.

I shoved him.

He fell back against the bed, clunking his head on the upper bunk. "Owww!"

I heard Mom coming. Before she got there, I leaped out the window. I had to get away from my dumb brother. He'd ruined my whole life. I couldn't stand to be around him another second.

Chapter 7

Alex Gets His
Nerve Back

I took a long walk. For hours I traipsed through the woods. I was so furious I hated every single thing around me. I threw a rock at a crow. I kicked my way through a large spread of lavender mushrooms. I broke a branch off an oak tree and smashed everything in my path. Maybe I'd just run away. I could hitch a ride north up to Oregon where my uncle lived. I could be around my cousins. They were all nice, perfectly normal kids.

Eventually, I got tired and came home. As I walked down the driveway, the Beast crowed at me from up in his tree. He was a macho guy — he didn't like to roost in the coop with the hens. I wished I was a big, strong, macho guy. But, even though I wasn't, I still didn't have to stay in the same room with my brother.

Mom tried to be the peacemaker. "Alex, listen to me. Nic feels bad about what happ—"

"Mom, you don't even know a thing about what he does to me. Everywhere I go, there he is to embarrass me. At school, on the bus, even in my own yard! I can't take it anymore."

"He doesn't mean to—"

"Mom, I don't want to talk about it." I marched to my room and dragged my pillow and blankets off the bunk. Bundling them up, I carried them out to the deck. I ate dinner out there by myself. I would never have anything to do with Nic again. I'd change my last name. I'd disown him.

I lay awake that night on the deck, awake for hours, making my plans on how to never be so humiliated again. First of all, I would stay clear of Nic. And, of course, avoid Brianna. I brooded about Brianna. I couldn't face her, but I couldn't forget her.

For a while, I actually succeeded in staying away from both of them. Despite Mom's objections, I rode my bike to school. I made sure I was nowhere near either of them at lunch or recess. On weekends I hung out with the Castro brothers or Jimmy. But one day I slipped up and had to deal with both of them again.

It happened like this. It was a Friday afternoon. Nic was bustling about with this goofy look on his face that I knew meant he was in a good mood. Goody for him! He was messing with his stupid voodoo box when I decided to take a hike. Maybe Jimmy would be home. But, just as I started walking up the driveway, guess who appeared?

Yeah. It was her. I froze. Classic Bambi-in-the-headlights pose.

"Hi, Alex!" She strolled toward me, like nothing had ever happened.

Speechless, I blinked. She was getting closer. Too late to run — wait a sec. What was I — a rabbit? After a second I found my voice. "Hi." I studied the bark on a nearby madrone tree.

"How's it going?" she said.

"Okay."

At that point, Nic came out. "Hey, Brianna!" he yelled. I've got some new stuff to show you. I found this dead cedar waxwing last week."

I stole a glance at her. She wrinkled up her nose. "Okay, Nic!" She smiled at me.

I couldn't help it. I smiled back.

"C'mon in, Brianna!" Nic called.

I decided to forget the hike. I pretended I was just going up to get the mail. After I returned to the house, I headed for the back room to read a book. Skellig. Weird title, good book. I ducked into the room and closed the door. Cowardly, I know, but certain actions take a build-up of nerve. It was very quiet. Mom had gone to the grocery store. Nic and Brianna must have gone outside. Anyway, as I re-read the same page for the umpteenth time, I realized it was hopeless — I couldn't concentrate a bit.

Finally, I crept into Mom's room and stood near the window, just behind the drapes. The garden is right below, and I could hear Brianna's voice. She was laughing. I hadn't heard that sound in a long time. I peeked out.

She was running up the pathway, trying to chase some of the chickens out of Mom's garden. Nic herded them along from the other side of the garden. The chickens scurried around the flower beds, stopping now and then to scratch at the soil and peck at the flowers. As I watched, a brown hen pulled a yellow pansy right out of the ground. Those flowers were Mom's new fall plants — she'd just finished planting them. I knew she was going to have a major hissy-fit when she saw this.

I figured I'd better get out there. I gave myself a little pep talk. Don't try so hard. Relax! You can't possibly embarrass yourself any worse than you did last time, but don't think about it. That's ancient history.

I grabbed a hotdog from the fridge and dashed over to the garden gate. It's supposed to be kept closed, but it was open now. I called "Here, chick-chick-chick!"

The chickens quit their mess-making and raced up the path and out through the gate. When they run, they stretch their necks forward and their feet fly out to the side, klutzy and funny.

Brianna jogged up behind them. "So that's how you get them out of there. What are you giving them?"

"A hotdog. It's their favorite food."

"Hotdog?"

"Uhuh."

Brianna watched the hens hopping around me, trying to snatch the bits of hotdog out of my hands. They're too plump to jump high — they only get a few inches off the ground before they plop back down.

Brianna giggled. "They look so silly."

"Yeah." I croaked out a little laugh myself. So far, so good. I tossed down the last of the hotdog and, in a minute, the chickens wandered off.

Nic came puffing up and the three of us stood there looking at Mom's garden. Pieces of pansies, snap-dragons, and zinnias littered the flower beds; their torn petals looked like rainbow confetti. Some of the plants lay upside-down, their roots sticking up in the air. Heaps of dirt made a mess of the pathway.

"Sorry we left the gate open," Brianna said. "I'll re-plant the flowers that got pulled up. Do you have a trowel?"

"I'm going to go make some ice tea," Nic announced and ambled off in the direction of the kitchen.

"Do you want some ice tea?" I asked Brianna.

"Sure." Her cheeks were pink from chasing the chickens around.

"Hey, Nic!" I called. "Make plenty, but go easy on the sugar!" I was talking to my brother again, at last. To Brianna, I added, "I'll go get some shovels and rakes. Be right back."

I went out to the shed to get the tools. In about ten minutes Brianna and I had the pathway cleared and the flowers were all back in the ground, right side up. Mom would never know.

Brianna pulled the hose over and began watering in the flowers. "So, Alex, Nic was telling me your little black hen is having problems hatching her eggs. How long has she been sitting on them?"

"Months."

"Months? I don't think it's supposed to take that long."

"Yeah, I know. She's got a ton of eggs but they're not doing anything." I wiped my dirty hands on my pants.

"Can I see her?"

We went to look. As we leaned into the darkness of the nesting shed, I could almost feel Brianna's shoulder touching mine. The air between us tingled.

Fluffy stared back at us, making these weird growling noises. *Grawwww, grawwww.* Her wings were spread wide and eggs spilled out from under her feathers. Her feet could hardly reach the hay because the eggs were piled so high. She looked like a tiny feathered queen atop a throne of eggs.

"Wow," Brianna said. "That's a lot of eggs."

"Yeah, I know. But she won't let me take any. And she can peck really hard." I rubbed a sore spot on my thumb where she'd nailed me earlier. I was just telling Brianna we better leave her alone, when Fluffy flapped and screeched at us.

Brianna jumped back, banging her head on the coop's door frame. The splintery wood snagged her hair. "Ouch." She tugged loose.

As I closed the coop door, I noticed a few silky dark strands dangled from the wood.

Rubbing her head, Brianna remarked, "I bet my cousin will know what the problem is. Daisy knows a lot about animals."

"Does she have chickens?"

"No, but one of our aunts raises animals and trains them. Daisy learned a lot from her."

We walked back toward the house.

"Actually, I should bring Daisy over some time," Brianna said. "I bet she and Nic would get along. They're a lot alike."

"Hmmm," I murmured. Sure, like my brother is even remotely similar to any other person in our species.

Brianna must have figured out what I was thinking somehow. "Really, Alex. They have a lot in common. I think Daisy would like to meet Nic and see his nature collection. She collects weird stuff too."

"She does?" I looked at Brianna.

"Yeah. I mean, she's smart and everything. Brilliant, actually, just like Nic, but..." Brianna shrugged. "She just kind of has her funny ways."

"Really." I slowed down my pace. "You think Nic's brilliant?"

"Well, he is. Obviously. His mind is like a computer — he knows all kinds of interesting stuff." Brianna looked at me earnestly. "You know, I like Nic. He's never mean and he always says what he thinks. Besides, he cracks me up. You never know what he's going to say." She paused and pushed a wisp of hair out of her eyes. "Nic's just so... so... himself."

I hiked my eyebrows up. Huh.

I think she would have gone on, but Nic himself came out. He slurped at a tall icy glass of tea. A sludgy heap of sugar sat at the bottom.

"Nic, I think Brianna wanted some too."

"Oh, my goodness. I didn't know that," Nic said. He thrust his glass at her. "You can have mine. It's not sweet enough anyway."

Yeah, he's just so, so himself alright.

Walking off, Nic announced "I'm gonna watch some TV now."

"Sorry," I muttered as I reached for Nic's glass.

"I'll just have some water," Brianna said.

"Sure." I went in and poured a tall tumbler of ice water. I cut up a fresh lemon from Mom's tree and floated a slice on the water. It looked about as good as a glass of water could. I made one for myself too and put a couple of not-too-stale cookies on a plate. I placed everything on a tray and considered whether I should add a vase with a few flowers. No, that might be overdoing it.

Taking a deep breath, I walked out, carefully balancing the tray. I noticed Brianna waiting at the picnic table, sitting in the shade of the huge fig tree. She was smiling at me. This was perfect, too perfect to last.

Chapter 8

Trouble with the Toad

Trouble sauntered down the driveway, with his hands in his pockets, acting like he owned the place. Todd the Toad.

I stopped so suddenly the water sloshed. Todd Hammerton never comes over here. Why did he have to show up at this moment? I set the tray down and walked over to him. "What do you want, Todd?"

"Now, now, Alexander. Where are your manners?" He smirked at Brianna. "You sure hang out with the strangest company, Brianna."

"I was enjoying the company. At least until a moment ago." She took a glass from the tray and sipped at the water.

"Oh, am I interrupting something special?"

"Todd, why don't you just leave?" Brianna stood up. Her eyes narrowed as she glared at him.

"Yeah, why don't you!" I said.

"I'll leave when I'm good and ready. I don't see any trespassing sign." He hawked up a nasty glob and spat it at my feet. It hit the ground with a wet splat.

"Gross!" Brianna said. "Look, Todd, Alex asked you to leave so will you please just go?" She folded her arms and scowled at him. "Now."

"Brianna! You used to be much friendlier. I guess these Stone brothers have turned your heart to stone." He laughed at his own dumb joke, the stupid hyena.

"You're trespassing." Her face flushed. She looked prettier than ever.

"Yeah, you're trespassing, creep," I added.

"Oh, Mr. High and Mighty! You've trespassed a few times yourself, haven't you?"

I knew what he was talking about. The lake. Thinking of the terrified ducks, I got furious. "You make me sick, Todd. Anyone who'd murder a bunch of baby ducks has got to be some kind of twisted pervert."

"What do you mean?" He crossed his arms and widened his eyes, all innocent-like.

"What *do* you mean, Alex?" Brianna asked.

I told her what'd happened at the lake. Todd kept interrupting, laughing and denying it. But Brianna believed me. Speechless, she looked at Todd like he was a mutant maggot.

"It's just his word against mine. He can't prove a thing," Todd remarked. "Can you, big guy?" he taunted as he towered over me.

Just then Nic wandered over. "Nothing on TV. Hi, Todd."

"Hi, dope. You and your brother sharing a girl-friend?"

That was it! "You're scum!" I bunched up my fists, but Brianna was faster than I was.

She dashed a big splash of ice water in Todd's face. That surprised him quite a lot. Me, too.

Then I noticed something coming up behind him, coming fast. Something big and mean with beady red eyes and huge sharp beak. It was the Beast.

I grabbed Brianna's arm and pulled her back. Nic was already backing up.

"Todd! Look out behind you!" I yelled. I couldn't stand Todd, but that bad-tempered Beast could get ugly.

He wiped the water out of his eyes and sputtered something nasty. Then he glared at me. "Do you really think I'd fall for that?"

"Todd! I'm not kidding!" I tried to warn him, but he didn't believe me.

"Bunch a little stinkin' babies, little scaredy cats!"

As he was gloating at the nervous looks on our faces, a screeching feathered fury slammed into his back. It clutched his shoulders. It pecked his head.

Todd screamed. He jumped around, swatting and yanking at the Beast, but that rooster really had his claws hooked in.

I glanced around, looking for the rooster stick. Anything. The hoe. I raced over to the shed, snatched it up, and dashed back to Todd.

He had shaken the Beast off his shoulders, but that crazed rooster was still after him. Both of them squawked loudly as they zig-zagged around the meadow. Todd twirled and kicked and hopped. He danced in terror. The Beast leaped and flapped right along with him.

I chased after the two of them. "Todd, wait! I'll get him away from you!"

But Todd was too busy dancing to pay me any attention. He kicked at the Beast and one of his sandals flew high in the air and caught on a tree branch. Eyes bugging out, Todd tore across the meadow.

I ran right behind him. "Todd! Stop!" He was headed straight for some thorny blackberry brambles. "Stay away from—"

He screamed even louder as he stumbled and tumbled into the thorns. The Beast had more sense. He stopped at the edge of the berry patch, flapping his wings and crowing. I waved the hoe at him and he strutted away, ruffling his feathers. He looked very satisfied.

Whimpering, Todd scrambled out of the brambles and hobbled for home.

In the quiet that followed, I heard some muffled choking sounds. When I turned around Brianna was collapsed against Nic, shaking with laughter. But Nic was not amused.

"Brianna, why are you laughing?" his voice rose, loud and shrill. "That wasn't funny — Todd got hurt. Didn't you see him bleeding?"

"I'm sorry, Nic,"

"You shouldn't laugh when someone is hurt."

"Sorry," Brianna said, biting her lower lip.

Nic stomped off to the garden, muttering.

"Guess I shouldn't have laughed, but—" Another giggle burst out of her. "It was just so... so—" She clapped her hand over her mouth and shook silently.

"I know, it was perfect justice! The Mighty Todd, rousted by a rooster!" I forced out a chuckle as I batted Todd's shoe off the branch. Someday, I'd give it back to him, but for now, I hung it on the chicken coop like a trophy. Even though I laughed, I felt uneasy. Knowing Todd, I was afraid he'd somehow have the last laugh.

Chapter 9

Alien Chickens?

"I've never seen anything like that rooster attack," Brianna said. "Todd's not really hurt that much, is he?"

"No, I think his pride got torn up worse than his hide." After I said that, I snorted at my own foolish rhyme and felt my face begin to burn. I've been hanging around with my wacky mom too long.

Brianna groaned and smiled, shaking her head. We walked over to the picnic table. As Brianna sipped at some ice water, she asked "What are you guys doing for Halloween?'

I shrugged. "Not much, probably. When we were little, we used to ride around the neighborhood in old Mr. Pike's pickup. He'd heap some straw in the back, and it'd be like a Halloween hay ride. It was great having a truck to haul our bags of treats."

"That sounds fun. It's such a bummer when you get too old to trick-or-treat," Brianna said.

"I know. So, what are you going to do?"

"I don't know." She fished out the slice of lemon and sucked on it. "I heard there's going to be a Halloween party at the community center. They're having a haunted house, music, games... Stuff like that."

I picked at some peeling paint on the table, gathering my courage. "Hmm," I said.

"Yeah, it sounds kind of fun." Brianna paused. "Well, I guess I better get going." She stood up, dusting off her pants. "Say goodbye to Nic for me, okay?"

"Sure." I cleared my throat. "That party sounds all right. I mean, if you like that sort of thing, it could be okay. You know, spooks and food and stuff."

Brianna cocked an eyebrow at me.

"I'll go, if you go," I blurted out. I couldn't believe how bold I was.

"Sure."

I beamed at her. Sure, she said. That wasn't so hard. "Hey, why don't you bring your cousin over tomorrow? Maybe she can help us figure out the egg-hatching problem. And we could plan our costumes too. We don't have much time left."

"Good idea. I'll call Daisy tonight," Brianna said. "What time shall we come?"

"Oh, anytime." I did some quick figures in my head. Definitely in the morning — I couldn't wait until afternoon. But not too early. I had to have time to get ready. "Well, how about ten?"

"Okay." She smiled. "See you then."

She headed up the driveway just like it was an ordinary day. I stared after her. This was just too good to be true.

I couldn't sleep that night. Mainly it was because of the wind. This time of year, the weather gets weird. First, cool like fall ought to be; then blazing hot. But the heat doesn't get to me like the wind does. It comes at night, rushing out of nowhere. It whips Mom's garden into limp shreds, knocks over the garbage cans, and rattles the timbers of our house. Last night the windows shuddered so loud I thought they'd break. Of course, Nic slept through it all.

In the morning I rolled out of bed at seven. I showered and washed my hair. Even rubbed in some conditioner — too much. Shampooed again. Mom yelled something about the well running dry so I got out.

I brushed my teeth until a foamy beard dribbled down my chin. What else? Deodorant? Why not? I grabbed a can of Mom's. Underarms, chest, back — all the sweaty parts. I would have done my feet, but the fumes from the deodorant got to me. Coughing, I fanned the air and stumbled out of the bathroom.

"Wheww!" Mom wrinkled her nose. "What—"

I shrugged and went into my room. I checked the clock — plenty of time. It was going to be one of those sweltering October days. Indian summer or whatever. I pulled on some shorts. My tan had faded. Maybe long pants. I fussed around with my clothes until Nic asked me why I kept changing them.

"Shut up," I told him. I was almost at the point where I could talk to him without wanting to strangle him. I checked the time again. One hour and fifty-seven minutes.

I tried to stay busy with chores to make the time pass, but it didn't help much. After I fed and watered the chickens and poured kibble in the cat's bowl, I sat out on the porch. Butter nudged my hand, reminding me she hadn't had her morning biscuit. I gave it to her and she lay down, drooling and crunching. It was still only sixteen minutes after nine. I had to find something to do. Since she was shedding, I decided to brush Butter. Five minutes later, I was covered with clumps of hair and smelled like a stinky old dog. Great, now I needed to wash up again. I hurried into the house. Someone was in the shower. Oh, no, not Nic! He always took forever.

I pounded on the door. "Nic, hurry up!"

"Okay!"

Twelve minutes later, he was still in there. Time to take action. I turned on the hot water in the kitchen. Full blast. A startled yelp came from the bathroom as the shower water turned cold.

"Okay, okay!" Nic yelled. The shower stopped.

I raced in, stripped off, and got wet. There wasn't much hot water left, but I gritted my teeth and soaped up anyway. I heard voices. Brianna and Daisy! I toweled off, threw on some clean clothes, and hurried out to the front porch. My hair was still dripping, but at least I smelled okay.

"Hi, Alex," Brianna said. "This is my cousin, Daisy."

"Hi, Daisy." I caught a flash of wide eyes the color of the first fresh grass of spring. Then Daisy turned to smile at Butter. Her sleek dark hair hung down, hiding her face. She reminded me of a shy fawn.

"Hi. It's very nice to meet you," Daisy said, holding out her hand.

She was still looking at the dog. I looked at her hand. I didn't know what else to do so I shook it. I guess that was the right thing because, after a quick squeeze, she pulled it back and crouched down to pet Butter.

"Where's Nic?" Brianna asked.

"I'll get him." I opened the door and called him.

In a minute Nic came out. Even though his shirt was inside-out, he looked okay. Clean hands, clear face, hair shiny as a polished penny.

"Hi, Brianna," he said. "Do you want to see my nature collection?"

"Uhhh, this is my cousin—" Brianna started to say.

"I want to see it," Daisy interrupted as she stood up. "Do you really have a mummified frog? I found a beautifully preserved alligator lizard under a sack of cement. It was flat and dry with only a slight lingering odor."

She didn't seem shy now.

"Really?" Nic answered Daisy. "Do you still have it? I'd like to see that. We could add it to my collection."

"Well, it's part of my collection, actually, but maybe we could trade. Do you have any complete mammal skeletons?"

"No, but I have two hummingbirds' nests..."

"Cool," Daisy said. Then she and Nic walked inside, chattering like old friends.

Huh! I stared after them for a moment. The screen door slammed and I turned back to Brianna. "Have you had breakfast yet?" I asked.

"Just a banana."

"How about some cinnamon toast?" I said.

"Sure. That sounds good."

We headed into the kitchen and I made my specialty — toast with butter, cream cheese, and lots of cinnamon-spiced sugar. "So, what do you want to be — for Halloween, I mean."

"I don't know. We'll figure something out."

Over the next few hours, we scavenged around the closets and the basement. Mom let us use some of her make-up and old things from med school. We came up with some good stuff. Brianna was going to be a mad scientist; I was going to be her monster. We decided we'd do a trial dress-up, just to see what we looked like.

Brianna gathered the things for her outfit and changed in the bathroom. I used my bedroom.

"I'm ready," I called as I smudged in the dark shadows under my eyes. My face was this gross shade of green — like the underbelly of a dead lizard — and I'd slimed my hair into greasy spikes. My clothes were just grubby old rags with some bloody-looking stuff splashed on them. I was trying to glue the metal bolts to my head when Brianna waltzed in and stood behind me.

"Deed you call for zee doctorrr?" she asked with a funny mad scientist accent.

"Zowie!" I looked at her reflection in the mirror. Her hair sprung out in frizzy corkscrews. She had drawn a huge red mouth around her lips. And her eyes!

"What did you do to your eyes?" I turned to face her and leaned close. Huge thick eye lashes and bright blue liner made her eyes look, well, weird. Definitely weird. She had a dark beauty mark on her chin that added a nice touch. In contrast to all that, she wore a professional-looking white jacket with a stethoscope hanging down the front. Her nametag pin said "Dr. BB Braindead." I chuckled. "That's good."

"Zen you approoooove?" Brianna crooned, waving a huge syringe like it was a cigarette.

"Yeah, it's awesome! What about me?"

Stepping back, Brianna placed one hand on her hip and stuck her nose in the air. "Vell, I zoopose zat veel dooo." She reached out to shove my wobbly bolt back into my temple.

Just then Daisy and Nic came tromping down the hallway. They stopped in the doorway and stared at us. "Cool! You guys look great," Daisy said.

"I want to make an outfit too," Nic said. "In fact, Daisy, let's go to this party. Do you want to?"

I stared at Nic. He'd just asked a girl he barely knew out on a date — his first date — and he made it sound so easy. Good grief!

"Sure! It'll be fun," Daisy answered. "What shall we be? I know — chickens. Let's go as chickens."

"Nah, too dull. How about aliens?" Nic suggested.

"I've got it — alien chickens!" Daisy said.

"Alien chickens? That's so weird. It's perfect. What planet should we be from?"

"Mars?"

"No, too predictable," Nic answered. They walked away, arguing about the most likely planet of origin for alien chickens.

I stared after them, feeling happy for Nic. And very happy for me. Finally, things were going our way.

Chapter 10

Chicken Expert Extraordinaire

Brianna and I changed out of our outfits and washed off our make-up. We sat out on the porch, sipping some lemonade.

"How do you like living up here?" I asked her. "Do you miss your old neighborhood?"

"I like it here." Brianna held out her hand and called, "Kitty-kitty," to Winks who was crouched on the porch rail.

The cat lashed her tail, annoyed; she was waiting for a careless bird.

"Mom says I could even get a pet now," Brianna continued. "In our old house, the landlord wouldn't allow it. Only problem is that Mom's real fussy about fur." Brianna started talking in a high-pitched bossy voice. "'BB, go change your clothes — you've got filthy animal fur all over them.' There was only, like, maybe two tiny hairs stuck on my shirt."

"So, what kind of pet do you want?"

"I don't know yet." She reached out to pet Winks, who ignored her. "It can't be furry or noisy or cause any kind of trouble. Mom's always fussing about something, especially now that my dad's gone." Brianna sighed and a shadow darkened her expression. After a moment, she asked "What's your favorite pet?"

"I used to have this cat, Cheyenne. He was nice. He liked to snuggle up and he purred really loud." I stopped and scratched at the dried glue on my face. "He got … got… the coyotes got him."

"Oh, that's too bad, Alex."

I felt that familiar choke in my throat so I started blabbing about our other pets. "Butter just sleeps. She's old and lazy. And Winks — well, you can see how friendly she is. She's such a stinky little savage. All she does is kill birds and set our house on fire."

"What?"

"It's strange, but true. Three times now. Once she knocked over the BBQ on the porch and the hot coals started burning the planks. Twice she decided to use the living room electrical socket for her own personal potty. Piss, sparks, fire. Just like that." I shrugged.

Brianna covered her mouth and tried to smother a giggle.

I laughed too. "I know this sounds kind of strange, but right now, I think our chickens are a lot more fun than the dog or cat. When you raise them from chicks, they can be tamed. Some of them are really friendly. I just wish Fluffy would hatch those eggs so we could have some chicks."

"Chicks — that's it! They're so cute. Besides, they have no fur." Brianna said, all bubbly and excited.

"Does your Mom use eggs much?" I asked.

"Yes! She'll have fresh eggs — I bet she'd like that." She gave me that hundred volt smile that always jolted my heart. "Are chickens hard to take care of?"

"Not usually. You do need to have a little coop."

"Oh. Do coops cost much?" she asked.

"Well, I don't know. I just built ours from a bunch of scrap wood."

"Oh…" She rolled the empty glass back and forth in her hands.

"I could help you make one. It's easy, really," I found myself saying. As if inviting myself over to do a project with Brianna Santos was the most natural thing in the world.

"Would you? That would be great," Brianna said. "When can we start?"

"Uhmmm…" I was crunching the last ice cube when I heard some angry cackling. "Something's bothering the chickens!" I leaped up and across the porch, hurtling a bucket of wood ashes. Down the steps and through the garden, I raced. I ran around the corner of the chicken coop and straight into Daisy and Nic.

"Yikes!" Daisy squeaked as the basket she held tipped. Several pale brown and green eggs spilled out. They landed with a messy splat on my feet.

Nic held his nose. "Peuwwww," he complained. "Major stink!"

"Ooops! Sorry, Daisy," I said, as I tried to wipe the sticky goo off with some straw. It really did stink. Those eggs had been sitting there way too long.

"Hey, Daisy, did you figure out why those eggs weren't hatching?" Brianna asked.

"It seems obvious, actually." Daisy carried the remainder of the eggs down the dirt bank. "Eggs need constant warmth to hatch, right? When there is an excessive number of eggs, such as we found in Fluffy's nest, the outer ones are not exposed to the radiant heat of the setting hen. Whoever is in charge of the chickens needs to take precautions against this occurrence."

She glanced my way and spelled it out so even a dope like me understood. "Don't let Fluffy set on so many eggs."

"That makes sense," I said. "But Fluffy's so protective. How did you get those eggs away from her?"

"It was easy," Nic piped up, waving Mom's favorite blue and white checked dishtowel. "I threw this on Fluffy's head and held it there, carefully, of course, while Daisy scooped up the outer ring of eggs."

"Yeah, easy," I agreed. I wished I'd thought of it a long time ago. We would have chicks by now. I followed Nic, Daisy, and Brianna back to the house. "When will the rest of those eggs hatch?" I asked Daisy, Chicken Expert Extraordinaire.

"Probably most of them will hatch within a few weeks," she answered. "As long as you follow the egg-hatching rules. Don't let any of the other hens lay their eggs in that nest now. Otherwise, the old eggs and new eggs will get jumbled and they won't get the proper heat and turning."

"Turning?" I asked.

"The hen has to move them around with her beak, turning them so the chick inside develops properly," Daisy explained. "You see, if — "

"Excuse me, Daisy, I think I get the idea. I really have to go wash my shoes now."

Brianna joined me as I hosed off my sneakers and put them on the porch railing to dry. "I guess I've learned the basic egg-hatching rules," I remarked. "Maybe we'll have some chicks soon." But, instead of having more chickens, by the next day we had fewer.

Chapter 11

A Dastardly Deed

That night I dreamed about chicks. Chicken chicks. (I don't call girls chicks; my mom told me it was rude.) Anyway, I was dreaming of cute fuzzy chicks when I woke up with a start. I thought I heard something.

The wind was howling, but something else woke me up. I lay there, listening. The wind paused, and I heard the frantic babbling of frightened chickens. I leaped out of bed, grabbed a flashlight, and raced outside. On the way up to the coop, I spotted the rooster stick. I snatched it up. There was no telling what I might find. Maybe a raccoon or skunk had got into the coop. Or maybe a coyote. I slowed down. I didn't want to meet any coyote up here in the dark. Mom had just read a story in yesterday's paper about a kid who'd been attacked by coyotes. Of course, that was in Montana. But still...

Cautiously, I peeked around the corner of the coop. The door had blown open. It was banging around, making a racket. Inside, the chickens squawked. Oooh, they were upset. I crept up to the doorway and pointed the flashlight inside. A dozen chickens blinked nervously at me, flapping their wings. The door flying open must have spooked them.

"Chickie, chickies," I crooned. "Nothing's wrong, you silly birds."

But something was wrong. As I closed the coop door, I noticed a heap of something underneath the rooster's tree. I shone the flashlight over there and saw feathers and blood. Oh, no! I edged a little closer. It was the Beast. He was dead. As I backed away, I tasted something bad in the back of my mouth. I'd take care of this in the morning. I'd tell Mom.

Back in bed, I huddled under the covers. I felt cold and my insides shook. I tried to go back to my dream about the chicks. But my mind kept flashing back to the Beast I knew and admired — the noisy, cocky way he strutted around. Now he was just a sad pile of bloody feathers.

It was a long night. Finally, morning came.

I told Mom about the Beast.

"But what got to him?" she wondered. "Why didn't it take him when it ran off?" She went out to see if his body was still there. In a few minutes, she was back. She had a look in her eye that I'd never seen before. "That was no animal that killed him," she told me. "Somebody shot him." She spat the words out furiously.

"What?" I stared at her. I couldn't believe it.

"Somebody shot him with a pellet gun. He's full of holes."

In a second I knew what had happened. Todd had taken his revenge. "I'm going to get him," I muttered. That lousy, slimy, glob of sewer scum. I hated his guts.

"Alexander Stone, you tell me what's going on. Now." Mom was mad. She made me spill out the whole story about Todd, Nic, the Beast's attack. Everything.

Then she got on the phone. "Mrs. Hammerton? Your son came trespassing last night and he murdered the Beast." Pause. "Our rooster. Yes, Todd shot him dead." Mom went on for a few minutes, explaining about Todd and the Beast; then she paused again. "What? But surely you—" Mom listened, drumming her fingers on the kitchen counter. "Well, no, but-" Mom's face got red as she listened. "Don't you worry!" She hung up the phone with a sharp click. "Oh, the nerve of that woman!" she sputtered.

She turned to face me, her hands on her hips. "Listen to me, Alex. That boy is a menace. And his mother is even worse. I don't want you to go anywhere near them."

I think Mom would have launched into one of her lectures, but luckily the phone rang. It was one of her mothers-to-be about to become a mother for real. Mom hurried out of the house.

I thumped around the living room, trying to figure out where to dump my anger. Nic bumbled out of the bedroom and down the hall. He yawned loud and long. It sounded like he was yodeling.

"Why are you throwing things around?" he asked me as he scratched his skinny belly.

"Todd shot the Beast."

"What? Our rooster? Why?"

"Because Todd's a cowardly creep and the Beast beat him up the other day, remember?"

"But he didn't have to shoot him," Nic protested.

"Well, he did."

"We should press charges against him. He must be prosecuted to the full extent of the law," Nic said, as he stood there in his underwear.

For once, I agreed with my brother. Todd had to be stopped. He was pushing this bully thing further and further. It was bad enough bothering Nic at school and shooting the ducks at the lake. But Todd had crossed the line. Now he'd murdered my rooster. What would it be next? And how could we stop him?

Nic's eyes glittered as he spoke. "We already know his motive — revenge. And he had the opportunity too, since he's our neighbor. He could've easily sneaked over here."

My brother was rambling on and on, as usual.

"We need evidence," Nic proclaimed, hands on hips. "That's the next step in this investigation."

Nic and his true crime stories! He gets carried away at times. But once in a while, he latches on to a good idea. If I'd been able to prove Todd was the duck shooter, maybe his little pellet gun would have been taken away. And this morning the Beast would be out there crowing up a storm.

"Like what kind of evidence?" I asked Nic.

"Foot prints. Bodily samples. Stuff like that." Nic was pulling on some shorts and shoes. "Let's go inspect the scene of the crime."

We went out and poked around the chicken coop. I noticed Mom had taken care of the Beast's body. A few feathers were all that remained of my rooster.

Nic spotted something. "Look!" he said, pointing to the doorframe of the coop.

"What?" I didn't see anything with Todd's name on it.

"Right here." My brother touched the wood. "See?"

I leaned close. There it was. Blonde hair. It had to be Todd's — no one else who'd been around here had light hair like his. This was practically proof. I tore a piece of paper from a feed bag, then plucked the blonde strand from the frame and wrapped it up. I wasn't sure exactly what I'd do with this wrinkled little package of proof, but I knew I wanted to do something.

"I'll be back in a while," I told Nic as I jammed the paper package into my pocket.

"Where're you going?" he asked.

"Out."

"You're not going to Todd's house, are you?"

I didn't answer. I was already half-way out the door. I tramped through the Christmas tree farm and up the ravine. The wind shoved big gray clouds across the sky and pushed against me. I leaned into it, marching towards Todd's house like a creep-seeking missile. The air was damp and chilly, but the heat of my anger kept me warm. It took me a while to go around Mr. Pike's pasture.

A devilish, yellow-eyed billy goat named Bonkers lived there. He must have been in the barn this morning, but I wasn't taking any chances.

Finally, I approached the Hammerton estate. I stayed hidden. Surprise was half the battle, I thought. The tangle of undergrowth gave me good cover, but it made the going slow.

I still didn't have a plan about how I'd handle Todd, but a vague idea was forming in my feverish brain. Maybe I'd tell him we had proof of his guilt and if he ever came anywhere near my brother or me or any of our friends or our pets…then, then, we'd — what did Nic call it? We'd push charges. We'd get him in so much trouble. We'd get him sent to juvie hall or someplace like that. That would fix him. Yet the plan didn't satisfy me. Whenever I thought of the duck family or my rooster, I just wanted to pound Todd's smug face into the dust. I didn't want justice; I wanted revenge. Blood. Too bad I'm such a weenie.

I reached the huge lawn that encircled the Hammerton's fancy mansion. A clipped hedge bordered the grass. I crawled along behind the hedge, homing in on my target. As I crept up to the brick patio, I could hear snatches of a conversation. Todd was getting into trouble. Good! He deserved it.

A woman's voice cracked like a whip. "How dare you? After all I've done for you! How dare you?"

I heard the sound of a slap. I winced.

"You've been nothing but trouble since the day you were born. I knew we should've sent you off to that boarding school. They'd shape you up." The voice rapped out some more nasty remarks and then was interrupted by a man's deep, growling voice. "Blah, blah, blah, no son of mine, blah, blah I'll bring out the Lasher blah blah!"

I couldn't catch all the words, but the low rumble was menacing. The Lasher? Oooh. I wasn't even the one they were going after and I was starting to get scared.

"Alex!"

I almost wet my pants. It was Nic. He was walking across the lawn towards me. Desperately, I shook my head and put my finger to my lips, shushing him.

Luckily, the discussion in the house was getting noisy. No one but me seemed to have heard Nic. The man was shouting now. "I'll teach you a lesson you won't forget anytime soon!" I heard a thud. Todd yelped. Then a crash. Holy Smoke! What was going on in there?

I decided Nic and I better beat it. This was obviously a personal family thing. I wiggled between a couple of boxwood shrubs, gesturing to Nic to go back, to hide, to scram.

He stood there in the open with a puzzled frown as he listened to the uproar coming from the house. Crouching, I ran along the outside of the hedge. Nic wasn't too far away from me now. And then, what luck! I came to a path. It was just a faint trail, but it seemed to lead where I wanted to go off into the woods.

"Nic! Come on!"

Finally, he got the message.

We raced along the twisting pathway. I heard a door slam back at the house. In a few moments, I heard footsteps, coming after us, coming fast and furious. We were busted!

Grabbing Nic's arm, I dove into some bushes. We huddled there, trying to still our breathing. Nic's chest heaved, but he was quiet, his eyes huge and dark with alarm.

Todd raced past us. I caught a glimpse of his face. It was twisted into a mask of misery. As we watched, he slowed down. He walked along the trail, scuffing his feet through the leaves, his hands clenched. He wasn't coming after us; he was just getting away from his folks. He headed for a fallen redwood tree about twenty yards away from us.

Don't stop there, I begged him silently.

He plopped down on the log. He started stripping the fuzzy bark, yanking on it and shredding it as he muttered furiously.

I couldn't hear what he was saying. And I didn't want to. I just wanted to get out of there. Nic started whispering to me. I hushed him and began slithering away through the underbrush. I took one last look at Todd.

I stopped.

My mortal enemy, the bully who'd tortured me and mine, slumped over with his face in his hands. Wheezing, choking sobs jerked his shoulders. I should have been glad to hear Todd Hammerton crying, but somehow I wasn't.

Neither was Nic. In fact, his freckled elf-face wrinkled in concern. He rose up to his knees and looked at me. "Todd's crying."

"Shhh. I know. This is our chance. Let's go." I started creeping away again.

"We can't leave him like this," Nic protested. "I learned in my ST group that it's important to try to comfort someone who is crying."

I was about to tell Nic that if he got near Todd now, he'd be the one crying. But, before I could grab him, Nic stood up and rushed towards Todd.

Chapter 12

Nic's Magic Chick

"Nic!" I gasped. "Come back here!" Somehow I didn't think Todd would be happy to see us right then. But my brother is clueless about that kind of fact. I really wanted to escape this mess, but I couldn't leave Nic. So I did what I could. I squatted behind a stump and watched.

At this point, Todd looked up. His eyes squinted, red and swollen. Strings of snot dangled from his nose. His mouth curled down in a puckered grimace. He didn't look like such a hotshot now.

As Nic got closer to him, I tensed, hoping Todd wouldn't knock my brother's silly head off.

Nic plopped himself down next to Todd, slung his arm around Todd's brawny shoulders, and said "Looks like you're having a real bad day."

I held my breath.

Todd drew back, staring at Nic, bewildered. After a few moments, he nodded, yes, and made this sort of strangled laugh. Then he started blubbering like a baby.

I couldn't watch anymore. I felt embarrassed just being there. I left. As I hiked home, I knew I'd seen the answer to something I'd wondered about for a long time. The why of Todd's nastiness. Now I knew he was just a regular kid — not a monster. His parents had pounded that ugly meanness into him. Even though I have a dead dad and a weird brother, I was way luckier than poor Todd. I pulled the crumpled packet of "proof" out of my pocket, dropped it, and scuffed some dirt over it.

About an hour later Nic shuffled down our driveway. "Todd's not going to bother us anymore," he said. "We're buddies now."

"That's good, Nic. That's real good." I wouldn't believe it until I saw it.

"Hey, look!" Nic pointed behind me. "Fluffy's off her nest."

"I guess that commotion last night got her a little upset," I said as we gazed at the little hen. She sat very still under the willow tree with her feathers puffed out around her. She kept sending nervous looks our way. "I'm going to check on the eggs, make sure the other hens aren't messing around in there," I said.

I hurried up the bank and crawled into the coop. I checked the nest. Oh, no! The eggs were all in pieces. First, the Beast, now this! Dang! We'd never have chicks! What had happened? Only one lonely egg was left. It sat back in a dark and drafty corner.

Nic yelled something. Something about chicks. "I know, I know!" I yelled back. "Something got them!"

"No, Alex! They're out here with Fluffy!"

"What?" I scrambled out of the coop and ran over to Nic.

"See? Watch this — they're going to pop out from under her wing."

I stared at Fluffy. Nic was right. Two little yellow fuzz balls peek-a-booed us. Then a black chick poked his head out and another yellow one with a few brown stripes. Their eyes sparkled like tiny black beads. It was amazing — yesterday, eggs; today, chicks. It was like... like... magic or something.

Nic and I crouched there together, both of us grinning like we were watching a circus.

After a few minutes Nic said "I'm going to go check and make sure none got left behind."

"I was just in there. There's none left; just an egg." I told him.

"Did you inspect it for signs of life?" he asked.

"Nic, it's just an egg, not an extraterrestrial life form."

"You never can tell," Nic scuttled up the bank, his hands flapping in excitement. In a moment, he returned, moving carefully, like he was carrying the world's most wonderful and fragile treasure. He held it up. "It's the last chick," he announced.

I looked at it. "Nic, that's an egg."

"Let's be precise, Alex. It's a chick inside an egg shell."

I touched it. It was stone-cold. "Nothing's going to hatch out of a frozen egg," I informed my brother.

"You never know." He headed for the house.

"What are you doing?" I called after him.

"I'm going to hatch it, of course."

"Oh, of course." This I had to see. I took one more look at Fluffy and her new brood, then I followed my brother into the house.

Nic knelt in front of the fireplace, holding the egg up to the heat. He whispered to it. "Come on, little chickie, you can do it." Gently he turned it over. "Come on. Don't give up."

This was pathetic. That egg was ice-cold. No way was it going to hatch. My poor dopey brother. He stretched out on the rug and watched the egg. He whispered encouragement. He really wanted that egg to hatch.

"Hey, I heard something, Alex!"

I didn't say anything. Nic's always hearing things. Still, what if...

I lay down next to him. I listened to him as he begged the egg to hatch. I stared at the egg. It glowed golden against the flames of the fire. I wondered if a chick really might be inside. What was it thinking? Was it all sad and discouraged being stuck in there like that? It gave me a creepy-sad feeling, thinking of a tiny chick slowly dying in that egg.

Oh, for gosh sakes! It probably wasn't even a live egg at all; I was probably feeling sorry for a glob of gooey breakfast food! I shook my head, snorting at my own foolishness.

Nic was still encouraging the chick, I mean egg. His eyes blazed, his fingers fluttered. His whole body practically vibrated with his effort.

Suddenly, I found myself whispering "Come on, you can do it!" Jeeeezzz! I couldn't believe it! I was talking to an egg.

The egg rolled. All by itself, I mean.

Chapter 13

Season of Sweetness

Nic grabbed me and hugged me. "It's alive, Alex. It's going to hatch."

"I know! This is incredible." I punched his shoulder, grinning like a goon.

We watched and waited. A crack appeared in the shell. Then a little hole. A beak poked out. After rocking around a bit, it lay still. "Is it okay?" I wondered aloud.

"It's just resting," Nic assured me.

For the next four hours that little chick pecked and squirmed and rolled its egg shell around. I felt tired just watching it struggle. It took a long, long time, but, finally, it wiggled out. This chick didn't look like the others, all fluffy and perky. This one was slimy and it couldn't even stand up.

"It doesn't look right," I said.

"It's just tired. It'll be fine," Nic said confidently. He made a little towel nest in front of the fireplace and tucked the chick in. It stretched out its neck and closed its eyes.

I crawled over to the couch and collapsed on it. Nic curled up on the rug, refusing to leave that chick. He used his arm as a pillow. I bunched up the quilt on the couch and tossed it over to him. Then I closed my eyes. It had been an amazing day.

Just before I dozed off, I started thinking about Brianna. Tomorrow I'd tell her all about the chicks. Maybe she could come over and... Halloween was almost here. We'd have such a great time together. My thoughts dissolved into dreams. Brianna and the chicks. Me and Brianna. Her face beamed with joy as I handed her such a special gift. She reached out to me and... and...

The next morning I checked on the chick in the living room. It looked a little better. Not wet and messy and naked, but still very weak. It lay sprawled against the fold of the towel. It blinked at me. I touched it. It felt like a scrap of lumpy velvet. It lurched up and tried to walk. Ah, oh. Its legs still didn't work. One was weak and the other was kind of curled up strangely underneath the chick. The little guy just wiggled in circles, spinning on its tail end. I watched it and felt a nasty squeeze of worry.

Nic came in with an egg on a plate and a cup of water. He cracked the egg — it was hard-boiled — and broke off a chunk. He began to chop at it with a fork.

"What are you doing?" I asked.

"Making breakfast. The chick needs to eat," he said.

"You're going to feed an egg to a chick? That's practically cannibalism."

"Eggs are perfect forms of protein," Nic informed me as he mashed the egg. "Besides, they're highly digestible and chicks love them."

Sure enough, the moment he placed the egg crumbs in front of that chick, it started pecking away like crazy. After it slowed down a bit, Nic dipped his finger in the water and held it out to the chick. As the drop trickled down off his finger, the chick caught it. It tilted its head back and swallowed.

"I don't know how this one's going to make it, Nic. It can't walk."

"It'll get better with a little help." Nic gently straightened out one of its crooked legs. As soon as he let go, the leg pulled right back into that weird curl.

"I wonder why it does that," I said.

"Probably wasn't turned enough when it was in the egg," Nic said. "Of course, getting chilled didn't help either. It might have suffered brain damage."

Great. I stared at this pathetic little ball of fuzz. How can a chicken hunt and peck if its legs and brain don't work?

"Nic, how do you know all about this stuff?" I gestured at the egg and water. "Wait, let me guess. Daisy White."

"That's right. You're fairly smart, Alex. For a neurologically typical person, anyway."

"What are you calling me? Never mind, I'm going to ignore that."

My brother smiled at me. "It's okay, Alex, you're fine just the way you are."

"Yeah, whatever." I stood up. "I'm going to see how the others are doing."

Fluffy huddled in her nest. Chickie noises came from beneath her feathers. *Peep-peep, peep-peep-peep.* The coop's gate banged against the post. I propped it back with a heavy stone. The wind was picking up, gusting harder and harder. Fluffy didn't care — after all those weeks of setting on her nest, she wanted some fresh air. She led her chicks outside, clucking to them. *Puk, puk, puk.* These chicks were strong. They dashed back and forth, hopping over sticks and pecking at the dirt.

I wanted Brianna to come over and see them, but Mom reminded me I hadn't done any chores yesterday.

Pooh! I scrubbed out the chickens' water bowls and spread some fresh straw in the coop. I loaded up the wheelbarrow with firewood and lugged it over to the back door. I stacked all the logs, tossing them impatiently. As I raked all the oak leaves into a huge heap, I breathed in the great smells of fall. Grapes ripening to raisins on the vine. The sweet wood-smoky smell of leaves turning crisp. Things could not hardly get better. Well, they could get a little better. Maybe Brianna could come over.

As I hung the rake back onto its rack, Nic came out on the porch. "Oh, boy!" He jumped right on top of my pile of leaves.

"Hey, I just finished raking these up, you dope!" Oh, well. I was in too good a mood to be really mad. I threw some leaves in Nic's face and dropped the rake next to him. "Here, you rake them up this time!"

"Maybe later. Will you give me a bike ride?"

I didn't answer. Instead, I ran to the phone and called Brianna. I was so happy and excited about everything, I forgot to be nervous. I actually sounded half-way intelligent. "I have a surprise for you," I told her.

"What is it? Tell me, tell me," she said.

"Come over and I'll show you."

The phone clicked. In ten minutes, Brianna trotted down the driveway. She spotted the chicks right away and went all googly-eyed over them. "Ahhh, they are just too precious," she burbled. "How many?" She started counting them. "Four?"

"There's one more, actually. It's got something wrong with it." As we walked into the house, I told her about the cold egg hatching.

Brianna bent over the crippled chick. "Oh, can I have this one?" She stroked it tenderly. "Hi, chickie. What should I name you?" She looked up at me. "Is it a boy or a girl?"

I shrugged. "I don't know if this one's going to make it." I really didn't want my first gift to Brianna to be a doomed chick. "Uhh, we should probably check with Nic."

She frowned and said "Don't worry. I'm going to take really good care of it. I know it will make it," she added, sounding fierce. She stared at me, daring me to say it wouldn't.

Oooh, she was touchy. "Okay," I told her. "You can choose another one too."

"Really?" She peered under the willow tree. Fluffy was smart. The branches drooped down low, like a leafy umbrella. They sheltered the chicks from the worst of the chilly wind and from the hungry hawks.

"I don't know, they're all so cute," Brianna said. "Will you pick one for me?"

"Oh, well, sure, I guess." I studied them carefully, considering. Finally, I pointed to the larger black chick. "That one's going to have beautiful feathers someday. They'll be so shiny black, they'll have green rainbows shining in them."

"Thanks, Alex. This is the best present anyone ever gave me." Brianna smiled at me.

Despite the goose-bumpy wind, I felt warm all over. If I looked her in the eye, for sure she'd know I was totally gaa-gaa over her. I scuffed some chicken poop off my shoe. "So, are you ready for the Halloween party?" I asked.

She nodded. "I can hardly wait."

But she did have to wait. And wait. And wait.

Chapter 14

A Slightly Menacing Undertone

At last! The night I'd been waiting for finally came. It was five o'clock, Halloween night. In two hours it would happen. I wouldn't be just a kid anymore — I'd be a...a... I'd be a real teenager. I'd have a date. And not just any old date. My first date would be with Brianna Santos.

I tingled all over. I could hardly stand the waiting. I tried to watch a Dracula movie, but I already knew it by heart. I checked on the chickens and made sure the gimpy chick was okay. It was starting to hop around, but it still couldn't keep up with the others. Maybe someday it would. Finally, darkness slid down like a black cloak. Time to get ready. I cleaned up, grubbed around for my monster outfit, and pulled it on. It was hot and kind of scratchy, but I wanted to be ready.

I was so ready. The feeling reminded me of when I was little, begging for my very first sip of Coca-Cola. When my folks drank it, something about the popping, fizzing sounds and rising foam made it seem so wonderful, so special. Like if you sipped it, you'd just float away. You know how dumb little kids are. Of course, tonight would be even more special than that. Much, much more special. Visions of Brianna danced in my head.

As I daubed on the mud-green face paint, I thought of her. I knew she was probably getting ready right now too. I hoped she was looking forward to tonight as much as I was. I gelled my hair and squeezed it into spiky shapes. Almost time to go. I could hear Nic thrashing around, trying to wiggle into his alien chicken outfit. I went into the bedroom to help him. I heard the phone ring and, a minute later, Mom broke into one of her ridiculous songs. This one was a take-off from The Wizard of Oz. "I'm off to catch a baby, a wonderful baby from God! La-la, la-la, la-la, la-lahh..." The wildly off-key warbling faded. She was probably digging in the closet for her birthing bag.

In a few minutes, Mom sashayed into the bedroom with her bag slung over her shoulder. "I just called Karen — she's going to drop you guys off at the party. And you can call her when you're ready to come home." Mom kissed Nic on the cheek and murmured "You look cute, Honey."

"Mom, cute won't cut it. I'm aiming for a mystifying appearance, with a slightly menacing undertone."

"Oh." Mom smiled. "Well, anyway, have fun!"

"Mom, answer me this — how do I look?" Nic asked Mom, his voice loud.

Ah, oh. He was getting worked up. He was so excited, he was starting to lose it.

Mom repeated the mystifying, menacing description and Nic settled on the bed, somewhat satisfied with the correct response. He plucked at his feathers nervously.

"And what kind of an appearance are you aiming for, Alex?" Mom asked me with a quick wink.

I just shrugged and grinned. I was too happy for words.

Mom kissed my cheek and whispered "Have a marvelous time, you marvelous monster."

"Uh, Mom, your lips are kind of green."

"Oh," she laughed, wiping her mouth. "I don't want to scare that baby back where it came from." She left. The front door banged as the wind caught it.

Boy, it was howling tonight. When a gust hit, it seemed to rattle every log in our cabin. I stepped out on the porch and looked up at the black sky. Perfect Halloween night. Wailing, the wind chased giant monster clouds across the full moon. Ghostly tendrils trailed behind. I stared up at the moon and it stared back. In a slightly menacing way, as Nic would say. I shivered.

I could barely hear the phone ring. As I opened the door, I heard Nic talking to someone. Then screaming at someone. He slammed the phone down and ran into our bedroom. Oh, no. I followed him down the hall. Bam! The door almost bonked me in the nose.

"Hey, Nic, what's wrong?" I called through the door.

"Leave me alone!" he yelled. I heard all this crashing and banging. Cautiously, I cracked the door open. Nic was trashing our room. Books flew into the window.

Shoes crashed into the walls. A huge stuffed panda almost knocked over the TV. I had to do something.

"Nic, stop!" I yelled over the uproar. Taking a deep breath, I walked over and put my hands on his shoulders. "Calm down," I said quietly. "Tell me what happened."

"Daisy's not going to the party. Says she has a stomach ache," Nic sputtered in outrage. "A stupid stomach ache! What a baby!" He yanked at his feathers, pulling fistfuls out and throwing them all over the floor.

Oh, Jeez! Why did this have to happen? Poor Nic. I looked down at him, slumped on the bed. Tears were starting to trickle off the end of his beak. Suddenly, I found myself saying what I really, really did not want to say. "Nic, why don't you come anyway? You can hang out with me and Brianna."

"That's a stupid idea. How would I look being the only alien chicken there?" Nic said.

"That doesn't matter. Come on. It'll be fun," I argued, trying to put enthusiasm in my voice.

"Nope. I'll just stay here." He began hurling darts at the dartboard. *Thunk! Thunk!*

I got out of the way. Normally, he was pretty accurate, but I wasn't taking any chances. I paused at the door, watching him.

"What are you looking at?" he shrilled.

I ducked out and yanked the door closed.

Well, I tried, anyway. Nic's big night was spoiled. At least my fun was still going to happen. But somehow, a bit of the evening's gleam felt tarnished. Restlessly, I roamed around the house. When was Karen going to get here? I was looking out the window at the trees waving wildly in the wind, when the lights flickered. Oh, great! Where was the flashlight? I grabbed it just as the lights went out. Nic started screeching like a werewolf was ripping his wings off. Nic really hates the dark.

"Nic! Turn on your flashlight," I yelled as I hurried down the hall.

"Where is it?" he screamed.

I opened the bedroom door. "It should be right there next to your pillow. Where it always is."

"It won't work, it won't work!" Nic muttered, banging it on the wall.

"Here! Take this one!" I handed him mine and went scouting around for another.

"Alex, don't leave me." Nic stumbled along behind me.

"I'm not, I'm not! Would you quit grabbing at my outfit like that?" I shoved his hand away. Where was that dumb babysitter? I didn't want to be late. Brianna would be waiting. And Nic was getting on my nerves. Seriously.

I brought out a couple of big fat candles and lit them. I wanted to goose the coals in the fireplace and toss in some logs, but I knew that plan would backfire. The wind was blasting so hard, for sure it would blow smoke right back down the chimney at us. Heavy smoke always gave me a headache and I was starting to get one already.

I flashed the light at the kitchen clock. A quarter past seven! That was it! I was going to call Karen and... and... I held the phone and jabbed at the button, waiting for a dial tone. A hollow raspy sound buzzed from the phone. I stared at it, stupid with shock. This couldn't be happening. I was supposed to be on my dream date with the girl I was crazy about. Instead, I was stuck in this nightmare babysitting my brother who was driving me crazy.

This was so unfair! I slammed the phone down. Calm down, Alex, I told myself. Karen is reliable. She is coming. She'll be here any minute.

Five minutes passed. Then fifteen. Maybe a tree blew down across the road. But a work crew would have it cut and cleared soon. Wouldn't they? I tried the phone again. No luck. When another half hour went by, I finally realized my evening with Brianna was not going to happen. Unless…

I stole a look at Nic. He seemed calmer now. Much calmer, really. He was just laying on the couch, shining his flashlight up at the ceiling. He'd pushed his beak up to his forehead. His face seemed pale. I wondered if he was sick. Nah, Nic never got sick. He was just tired. His eyes drooped.

It would take me about twenty minutes to sprint down to the community center. Brianna would be waiting, maybe a little mad, but I'd explain what happened. She'd forgive me. I was almost sure. But how could I get out of here without Nic throwing a fit?

I drummed my fingers on the counter, thinking. There had to be a way. I snapped my fingers. That's it!

Casually, I strolled over to our emergency radio and began fiddling with the dials. I found a jazz station. Real mellow music, sleepy-time stuff.

"I don't feel like music," Nic announced.

"Well, there's nothing else to do," I reasoned with him. For once, he listened to reason. All the energy seemed to be drained out of him. I sat in the rocker and watched him out of the corner of my eye. His body sagged. His eyes fluttered and closed. His lips quivered with little puffs of air. He fell asleep. Perfect.

I'd dash off to the party. I'd tell Brianna what happened. I'd promise to make it up to her somehow, someday soon. And then I'd race right back home. I wouldn't be gone long. An hour, max. Nic would never even know he was alone. And what he didn't know, couldn't hurt him. Right?

Chapter 15

The Howling

I eased out of the rocking chair. It creaked. I froze as Nic flung his arm over his face. I waited for his breathing to deepen again. Once Nic fell asleep, he usually conked out. It would take a locomotive roaring through the living room to wake him.

Holding my breath, I tiptoed to the front door. With one last look at my brother, I slipped out of the house. I stood on the porch, almost panting with nervousness. This could work. What could go wrong? I hurried down the steps and then stopped. What was I thinking? The candles! If they burnt too low, they could burn up the house. And Nic too. Holy smoke! How stupid could I get?

I retraced my steps, hurrying now, before I lost my nerve. I blew out the candles and was out the door in a flash. Hurry, run, you fool! As I leaped off the porch, my foot hit something. *Rattle! Crash! Thunka-thunka- thunka!* The bucket of wood ashes clattered down the steps.

Dang it! I stood there, holding my breath. Sweat ran down my face. Not a sound from the house. I waited, expecting Nic to blast out the front door. He didn't. Just to be sure, I sneaked back to the door and eased it open. Just a crack. Nic was laying on the couch. He hadn't moved a muscle. I closed the door. The latch fell into place with a quiet snick.

I leaned my back up against the door. A fit of giggles got hold of me. I clapped my hand over my mouth, snorting and snickering. My nerves were shot.

Suddenly, the door gave way. As I fell backwards, a scream almost shattered my eardrums.

"Aghhhhh!"

"Aghhhhhh!" I shrieked back.

"What are you doing?!" Nic hollered.

I looked up into the face of an angry alien chicken.

"I... I..."

"You were going to ditch me, weren't you? Some brother you are! You were going to just leave me here alone, right?" Nic started ranting and raving. "Just so you could go play kissy-face with Brianna! You wish you could get rid of me, don't you, Alex?" He leaned over me, spitting in his rage. "You hate me, don't you? Go ahead! Say it!"

"Shut up, Nic."

"I've ruined your life! You hate me, don't you?! Say it!"

"Get out of my face, Nic!" He's so melodramatic when he gets going.

"Not until you say it!" He plopped down on my chest.

I squirmed and bucked under him. "Get off of me!"

"Say it!" He bounced and the breath burst right out of me.

I grunted in fury and shoved at his chest. I couldn't get him off. "Okay," I growled. "I hate you! You're a brainless, selfish jerk and... and I wish you would just disappear. Forever!"

Nic lurched to his feet and ran to his room.

I was so mad I felt like chasing him down and pounding him. I stomped out the door instead, muttering and cursing. I do hate him! I do! That stupid punk! I marched out to the orchard, kicking dirt clods and calling my brother every evil name I could think of. I slipped on an apple, twisting my ankle. The pain made me even madder. I started snatching up apples and hurling them against the tree trunks. Splat! Splat! Splat! I must have mashed a hundred perfectly good apples into apple sauce.

In the distance, a coyote yipped. After a while, I went back to the house. It was quiet. Nic must have fallen asleep. I tried the phone again. Just a loud hiss. The party was probably almost over anyway. I hoped Brianna wasn't too mad at me. A wave of sadness and exhaustion rolled through me. Why'd this have to happen? Why'd I have to say that to Nic? It wasn't his fault. It was just... just... the way things were.

I wiped my monster paint off and pulled off the dumb monster jacket. Quietly, I padded down the hallway. The litter from Nic's tantrum still lay all over the floor. Magazines, model planes, pillows, darts, Nic's nature notebook.

I started to scuff the notebook out of the doorway, when it flipped open and I saw my name scribbled on a page. Nic had always been careful to keep his notebook tucked away. I couldn't understand why — who cared? It was just a bunch of rambling on about bugs and lizards and weeds and stuff, right? So why was my name in there? I knew I shouldn't read his personal stuff, but I was curious now. What did he write about me?

I picked the notebook up and smoothed out the wrinkled pages. I scanned the flashlight over them. Hmmmm. A lot of writing. Some drawings. Even a few old photos. This was not what I thought it was. This was...

I peered closer, whispering the words. I couldn't believe what I was reading. Words of beauty and passion glowed on these messy pages. It was like poetry, magical and graceful. Here was Nic's sorrow and his fury, his joy and longing rising up from the pages like the dawn mist on a still pond. I knew this was very personal. I knew I should snap the notebook closed and drop it back on the floor. But I couldn't.

Instead, I clutched it close to me and tiptoed back to the living room. I stretched out in front of the fireplace and opened Nic's private pages.

Page one. The date was five years ago. Shortly after Dad died. I started reading. After a page or so, I almost stopped. Something strong was squeezing inside my chest. I read some more. Nic's struggle to accept Dad's death was every bit as painful as mine; he just never talked about it. Or maybe he had tried to tell me. Why hadn't I listened? I was too busy feeling sorry for myself, I guess.

I studied the photo pasted in there. Dad was cradling Nic in his arms, smiling tenderly at him. Nic was leaning way back, gazing skyward with wide-eyed fascination. I sighed and turned the page.

Nic seemed to turn to nature to get away from his sadness. He described following a butterfly around all day, watching what it did, wondering how such a delicate creature could fly in the face of a strong wind.

Further down he wrote "Some people think I just drift around aimlessly. But they don't know. 'Not all who wander are lost.'"

There was a story in there too. A sci-fi fantasy about another planet, a place where the inhabitants were weird bird-like humanoid creatures. Nic focussed on their grace in flight and how marvelous a feeling it would be to fly.

Here was a portrait of Nic and Mom. A colorful pastel sketch of them laying in the grass, arms and legs spread-eagled, staring up as rainbow clouds swirled in dizzy circles. It was captioned: "And the blue sky spins all around, all around; And the blue sky spins all around." Probably one of Mom's crazy songs.

There it was. My name. Nic wrote how he wanted to be like me, strong and brave. How if only he could ride a bike like I did, he would know what it was like to fly. Me, strong? I was wiry, I guess, but still muscled like a mouse. And brave? Hah! That was a regular laugh riot.

I leafed back and forth through the notebook and spotted another photo. This one showed Nic and me when we were toddlers. We were splashing each other in a kiddie pool, eyes squinched shut, mouths wide open, laughing. It was labeled "Me and My Best Buddy." Hmm.

I pored over the pages, pondering their meaning. Some of it was so far out, I just shrugged and skimmed over it.

Then I came to some recent entries. There was a list of Nic's friends, a short list. The bus driver, his teacher, and Brianna. Todd's name was squeezed in. So was Daisy's. Mine was crossed out.

Below, it said "I'm such a dope, no one wants to be around me. My eyes won't zero on faces like they're supposed to. And my hands flap, driving people away. I'm such a moody motor-mouth, even Alex is sick of me. I'm sick of myself."

The flickering flames were making my eyes burn. Gently, I closed the notebook and put my head down on my knees. I scrubbed at my blurry eyes.

Sometimes I felt like a two-hundred pound Vulture of Sadness was sitting on my shoulder, digging in deep with its claws. No escape. It would always be there, waiting.

How could I be so mean to Nic? Wasn't his life tough enough? He was really an amazing person. I was lucky to know him! I chewed on the inside of my cheek. And I do love him. Even when I can't stand to be around him, I still love him.

I lay back, pulling the quilt up and settling my head back on my clasped hands. I'm going to be a better brother, I resolved. Tomorrow, I'll take Nic for a ride on my bike. Tomorrow, I'll show him how great it is to fly. Tomorrow...

The wind battered the house. The timbers groaned. Flurries of leaves and acorns pattered on the roof, sounding like rain and hail. I closed my eyes. I don't know how I fell asleep with all that racket, but I did. It was the silence that woke me.

I jerked awake. My heart was thudding. It was so quiet. The wind had quit. Then, an eerie howl split the silence. And another. A third time. They burst into an unholy chorus of ugly yaps and sharp cries. Coyotes on the prowl. The wailing sounded so wicked, it made my skin quiver like a snake was crawling up my spine. When they all yipped and yodeled like that, it seemed like cruel laughter, taunting their prey. You can't get away, they seemed to say. I could just picture their teeth slashing some poor animal to bits.

The howling sounded closer, maybe they were chasing something down the gully that ran behind the house. I pulled the covers over my ears. Jeez! When would those beasts shut up? I'd never heard them come so close before. What were they after? I trembled, listening to them. I sweated in fear. Why wouldn't they go away?

Chapter 16

Cornered

Finally, the coyotes quit their hideous wailing. Everything hushed.

I sighed. What a relief. Then, as I closed my eyes, a new sound floated through the darkness, a sound that sucked my breath right out of me. A high, thin, wavering call.

"Here, chick-chick, chickie!"

Was I dreaming? This had to be a nightmare. I listened, disbelieving.

"Here, chickie!" It was no nightmare. It was Nic.

Nic was what the coyotes were hunting! For a few seconds, absolute horror paralyzed me. I turned into an ice statue. I couldn't breathe. Then, I exploded off the couch. A scream rose up from the bottom of my stomach. "Nic!" I roared as I flew out the door. "Nic!"

Frantically, I scanned the dark forest. A pinprick of light bobbed in the woods up near the gully. Nic and his flashlight. "Nic, the coyotes are coming!" I screamed.

What-to-do? What-to-do?! I spotted the tall, jagged silhouette of Fluffy's favorite roost. I sprinted uphill towards that tree, running fast as I could and yelling "Nic, climb Fluffy's tree! Climb the tree!" I reached the hilltop and dashed across the meadow, stumbling over the gopher mounds.

Swish, swish. The rush of bodies through the bush. Eager panting. Claws scrabbling on rock.

They were closing in on Nic. I had to get to him first. Had to!

I could see his flashlight swinging as he ran through the forest. I barged straight through a thicket. "Have to get there first," I panted. "Have to. Have to."

Branches whipped my face, almost blinding me. "Nic," I sobbed. Each breath seemed to rip out of my chest. The picture of Nic being torn apart flashed through my mind. I couldn't let it happen! Moonlight and shadows whirled around me like a crazy kaleidoscope of horror.

"Climb Fluffy's —"

Excited yips and snarls interrupted me. They were too close. Nic couldn't climb the darn tree anyway and I'd never reach him in time! I cried out in despair and tripped on a fallen branch. As I slammed into the ground, my breath was knocked right out of me. Somehow, so was my terror. Fury replaced fear. Gasping, I leaped to my feet and snatched up the branch.

"NOOOOOOOOOO!" I bellowed as I charged into battle.

The coyotes had Nic cornered, his back against the tree. They darted around him, jaws dripping, fangs gleaming. Three of them. A big one. Two smaller.

"Get away!" I raged. I launched myself at them, swinging the branch like a baseball bat. Crack! Right in the ribs. Yelp! They scattered. Whining cowards!

I backed up against Nic. I crouched down. "I'm the bench, Nic! Climb the tree!"

He scrambled on top of my shoulders. I strained to stand up. My muscles bunched up. They burned.

Fangs bared, the coyotes circled closer. They saw their chance. As they darted toward me, their yellow eyes glowed.

Darn devil dogs! I struggled to stand. "Back!" I gasped.

They leaped at me, snapped, snarled.

I snarled back. Poked that one. In the mouth. Rapped another. Right on the nose. Then Nic's weight was off me. I straightened up.

Now what? They were getting bolder. I lunged at them, brandishing the bat. I swung it at one, but another slipped behind me. I heard its teeth click in the air as I spun around. Nailed him. Ha!

Then pain seared my rump. Yeowww! He got me! I was in trouble now.

The taste and smell of blood drove them into a vicious frenzy.

Desperate, I started swinging wildly. I sobbed like a baby. I was a goner, for sure.

Nic yelled something.

Duck? I ducked.

A light flashed by me. Banged the big coyote right on its head. *Thunk!* It staggered for a moment, shaking its head. Then it went down, its eyes rolling back, lathered tongue lolling out. The others sniffed at the downed coyote, then, whimpering, scuttled off into the darkness.

I stood there, gasping for breath. I stared. "Way to go, Nic! Bull's eye!"

"Are you okay, Alex?" Nic called down to me. His voice wobbled.

"Yeah, basically, I'm okay."

"Good, that's good," Nic said. "He's okay. I'm okay. We're all okay." Then he pulled something out of his pocket and leaned over, handing it down to me. "The wind blew the gate open and he got lost."

"What?" I mumbled. "Who?"

"Here," Nic said.

Keeping my eye on the fallen coyote, I held out my hand. A piece of dandelion fuzz landed in my palm. *Peep-peep-peep.* It was a chick. My brother had gone out into the darkness he feared, out into that wild wind-storm, for a chick. He'd almost got himself — and me — torn to bits, for a chick. A sickly, gimpy chickie.

Peep-peep, it cheeped, blinking at me.

I cupped the chick in my hand and started chuckling. It wasn't funny, but it was. "Let's get out of here," I sputtered.

Nic slid down out of the tree. We backed away from the coyote and scanned the forest for the others. No sign of the cowards. We high-tailed it for home. I clapped my hand over my butt and winced with every step.

Through the darkness of the woods, the back porch light glowed a welcome.

"Look, Nic! The power's back on!"

After we put the chick back with its mother, we locked up the gate. We dragged an extra heavy log in front of it. It wouldn't get blown open again. Then we trudged into the house.

Mom was still gone. This was good. No need for her to see us like this, all bloody and muddy. And chilled. I couldn't stop trembling. Hot showers and soft pajamas would feel so good. Some aspirin wouldn't hurt either.

The shower helped get rid of my shakes, even though it burned my bit-up butt. I finished toweling off.

"Hey, Nic, would you plaster this on me?" I asked. I slathered a large band-aide with antibiotic ointment and handed it to him.

"Sure," he said. He peered at the wound. "Oooh, that's got to hurt. Bet you're going to need stitches."

I groaned.

Gently, he bandaged the wound. "Probably rabies shots too."

"Wonderful," I moaned as I eased my PJs up over my sore rump.

"Alex, I'm sorry." Nic stood in front of me, looking me straight in the eye. "I'm so sorry."

"For what? You nailed that coyote and saved my hide — most of it, anyway," I told him, smiling. "You did good." I punched his shoulder gently.

"I mean, I'm sorry for everything. You know… I'm not the easiest brother to be stuck with." The skin around his eyes got this purple-plum color. His eyes glistened.

"No, Nic, it's not like that. Not at all like that." I started blinking. Nic's face blurred. "Nic, you are the best brother in the entire world. The best!" I had to choke the words out. "And, I wouldn't trade you for anything." I wrapped my arms around him and hugged him so hard he squeaked. "I love you like crazy, you dope. You better not ever forget it." I meant every word of that, too. My brother, Dominic Stone, had a hero's heart beating in that scrawny little chest; he was true and brave in all the most important ways.

Nic hugged me back. "Ahhh, Alex…"

That's when Mom walked into the house. "Hi, guys," she called. "What are you doing up — " She stared at us with our arms around each other. A sweet mama-smile blossomed on her face. Then, she caught sight of the bloody clothes heaped on the floor. "Ah, oh." Her smile faded to a worried frown. "I think you two have some explaining to do."

We started to tell her about our adventure. When we got to the part about the coyotes cornering us against the tree, Mom said. "Hold it. I'll be right back." She returned with a glass of wine. She sat down on the couch, took a gulp, and shuddered. "Okay, you're surrounded by a pack of —"

"It was only three, Mom." I had to calm her down. Mothers get shook up so easy.

Mom narrowed her eyes at me. "Only three vicious, hungry, possibly rabid coyotes." She sipped at her wine, squeezing her eyes closed tightly. "And, my sweet darlings, how did you get out of that mess?"

We told her, keeping it short. Mom had to inspect the damage to my rear end. "Well, it's almost dawn anyway. Why don't we try to catch a few winks now. I'll call the doctor when we wake up."

We nodded. Now that the excitement was over, I felt like I could sleep a year. At least.

I let Nic have the top bunk. I crawled into his bunk, lowering myself carefully down on my belly. I don't even remember closing my eyes. When I woke up, the sun streamed through my window. Memories of last night flashed through my mind. I had to call Brianna!

Chapter 17

Golden Hearts
Raining Down

I sat up and a burning flash of pain stabbed my rear end. Gingerly, I eased out of bed. Yeowie!

I hobbled over to the phone. It worked this morning. But when I called Brianna, Mrs. Santos answered. "She's in school right now," she told me in a huffy voice.

I could hear her thinking "Why aren't you?"

"Uhh… " Duh. Of course, she was in school now.

"Is this Alex?"

The way she said my name she made it sound like I was a Brand X pimple cream that no one would want to buy.

I admitted it was me. It was too long to explain why I wasn't in school, so I just said "Would you tell her I called?"

She paused. I mind-read again. It was ugly. "Why did you stand up my daughter, you nasty little rat-fink?" she was thinking.

Aloud, she answered me with a grudging "Hmf. Okay."

In a while, Mom and I dropped Nic off at school and drove down the mountain to the doctor's appointment. After half a dozen stitches and one giant shot in the caboose, I was ready to crawl back into bed. Hearing that I needed a whole series of rabies shots didn't make me feel much better either. I was glad to doze off and forget everything for a while.

When I woke up, it was dark. It was hard to even figure what day it was. I had no idea what the clock said, but I knew it was definitely time to call Brianna. Dry-mouthed, I dragged myself to the phone. It rang a long time.

Finally, Brianna's mother answered. "Brianna went to bed hours ago," she told me. "And she waited hours out in front of the community center last night." As she banged the phone down, I heard her mutter something about that wacko family. I'm pretty sure she meant us.

Mom wouldn't let me go back to school for a few days. Since I felt sore and battered everywhere, I didn't complain much. But I had to talk to Brianna. Whenever I called, Mrs. Santos said she was busy or not there or something. After a while, she told me to stop being a pest. I wrote a note explaining what happened. Nic was going to deliver it, but he came down with the flu and had to stay home.

Finally, I returned to school, still sort of gimping along. I looked for her all day long. Once, while I was searching out in the back playing field, I came across Todd.

"Hey, Alex! How's it going?" he called.

"Good." I kept walking, too surprised to say more. I'd had too much on my mind to think about him lately. Maybe Nic was right about making peace with him.

Finally, I caught a glimpse of Brianna, but she was on the far side of the school grounds. She flitted through the crowds of kids, elusive as a dream. She didn't ride our bus that day. She was busting my heart into a million smithereens. I had to talk to her.

After school, I hobbled down the road to her house. I knocked. No one answered.

I shuffled towards home, hands in my pockets. What was I going to do? I heard a twig snap and looked up in time to see a glint of dark eyes.

"Brianna!"

She glowered at me. "I waited all night for you! Everyone laughed at my dumb outfit — they thought I was a dental assistant." Her voice raised to a squeaky pitch. "I can't believe you did that to me."

"Brianna — " I started to explain.

"I never want to see you again!" She flicked something out of her eye and tossed her head. "Never!" She turned and bounded down the path that led to the lake.

"Wait, Brianna! Please!" I limped along, my haunch burning. When I came to that chain link fence, I knew I couldn't climb it today. No way. I looked up and down the stretch of chain links. Aha! There was a little hollow. Whimpering, I scooched under the fence on my belly.

I tried to hurry down the trail toward the lake, but my legs wobbled. I couldn't go much further. I paused and bent over, resting my hands on my knees. "Brianna!" I called hoarsely.

"What's wrong with you?"

My head snapped up. I stared at her. She perched on a boulder above the trail.

Peering down at me, she frowned. "Are you hurt?"

I nodded, giving her a feeble smile.

She climbed down and stood before me. She crossed her arms. "What happened?" she asked, daring me to come up with a good story.

I licked my dry lips. "It's a long story. Can we sit down in the shade somewhere?"

"I guess so." She eyed me suspiciously. I'm not sure she believed anything I said.

As I took a shaky step, she asked "Does this long story have something to do with why you stood me up on Halloween?"

"Yeah."

We tramped slowly through the eucalyptus grove, slipping over the long crackly leaves and shaggy strips of bark. The path sloped down and the soil got sandy and soft. We came to a boggy area. Willow trees and poplars grew thick through here. The only sounds were the leaves rustling in the breeze and a dove cooing softly. And my breathing.

I panted, but I didn't whimper. The pain faded as my mind zeroed in on the hope that maybe Brianna would forgive me.

She wasn't saying much. Nothing, actually. If I could just explain properly… I was feeling kind of dizzy. I paused, glancing skyward for inspiration. "Nice day, huh?" I mumbled.

Staring at me, she raised her eyebrows. "Would you just tell me what happened?"

I looked away, my face burning. "Let's sit over there." I gestured to a huge fallen log near the water. Actually, sitting down wouldn't work. Moving with great care, I lay down on my stomach. Twisting my neck, I looked up at her.

Brianna stood, silent as stone, staring out at the lake.

Nervous, I fiddled with some leaves on the log. Then I started my story. By the time I got to the part about the windstorm blowing down the phone lines, Brianna was looking at me. When I got to the part about trying to sneak out without Nic, she'd sat down next to me. As I described fighting off the coyotes, she bit her lower lip and her eyes got bigger and bigger.

When I finished, she sat still, wordless. Finally, she murmured "I am so happy you and Nic are okay." Then she started to say something. "I'm, I'm…" she stammered. "I'm sorry I was being mean. I just thought…" She shrugged. "I don't know what I thought."

"It's okay. It's no fun to be stood up."

"Yeah." Brianna twiddled a long strand of her hair with nervous fingers. "My dad's only stood me up about a hundred times. He always says he'll come and take me someplace special, but then…" Her jaw tightened.

The look on her face made me want to put my arm around her shoulder, shelter her from her sadness. Instead, I looked at the leaf in my hand and traced the delicate veins with my finger.

Some more leaves fluttered down and Brianna caught one as it twirled past her. "Hey, it's raining golden hearts," she said, holding the heart-shaped leaf in her palm.

I gazed at the leaf. She was right. "Hmmm. I never noticed that before."

Her hand lay so close to my face. I looked at her finger nails, smooth and pearly, like tiny sea shells.

I felt incredibly tired all of a sudden, but tired in a good and peaceful way. I lay draped on that log with Brianna smiling at me and that turquoise lake shimmered so brightly that my eyes teared up at the brilliance. Blinking, I thought I saw something move.

"Look! Over there, on the far side," I said, pointing. "What is it?" We watched something flying along a wooded gully, swooping through the trees like a silver ghost.

Finally, it soared out across the lake. It was a great blue heron. It cruised over the water, its long neck and legs stretched out gracefully. Then, it rose and soared away, out of our sight. Something inside me, something heavy and sad, lifted and sailed away too.

I closed my eyes. This day was turning out too perfect for words, turning into some kind of magical day that you might just have once in your life. If you're lucky. I didn't realize how lucky we'd be until something almost ended us.

Chapter 18

The Gift of the
Midnight Star

After the recent windstorm, it seemed especially quiet. The breeze quit and the air felt breathless. Brianna and I walked back the way we'd come. I moved slowly, but the pain from that bite didn't seem to hurt so much. The only sound was our footsteps squishing through the boggy soil. We passed through the golden heart trees — they'd never again be just poplars to me.

As we followed the path through a cluster of scrub oak trees and coyote brush, the quiet exploded. A whirring buzz surrounded us. Brianna and I jumped a mile high as a large covey of quail burst out of the bushes next to us. The plump birds zoomed away, chittering in alarm.

We laughed at each other.

"Wow, that about gave me a heart attack," Brianna said, fanning her face.

"Me too." Boy, was I ever jittery. I'd only surprised a zillion quail in my life. They'd never spooked me like that. What was wrong with me?

We hiked onwards. Ahead loomed the shadowy grove of eucalyptus trees. When we reached them, we paused. The thought of clambering over all those big fallen logs didn't appeal to me right then.

I was thinking maybe we should circle around the grove and follow the lakeshore when Brianna asked me something. "How tall do you think these trees are?"

We craned our necks and looked straight up into their branches.

"I don't know. Maybe a hundred feet or something."

The gigantic trees towered over us. Even their branches were enormous. Standing beneath them, Brianna looked like a tiny forest sprite.

"C'mon," I said, looking back over my shoulder. The absolute stillness of everything was making my insides quiver. We walked into the shadowy forest of eucalyptus, climbing over fallen branches, and edging around old stumps.

Something creaked loudly.

What was that? I peered into the gloom. It's nothing, you little wussie.

But it was something.

A few minutes later, when we were deep inside the grove, something happened.

One second, all was fine; then, a sound like a cannon ripped through the stillness. A deafening blast seemed to crash at us from all sides. Brianna and I spun around, looking desperately for whatever was happening. We looked up at the same time.

Far, far above us, a gigantic branch, big as a telephone pole, was wrenching free from a tree trunk. It tore loose, swung around, smashed and bounced against other branches.

"Run!" I yelled, pushing Brianna along ahead of me.

A storm of branches roared down around us. We started to dash one way, but the monster branch swung after us. It battered everything in its path.

I grabbed Brianna's hand and we dashed the other way. As we scrabbled over the woody rubble of the forest, the noise sounded like a herd of elephants chasing us. We shoved frantically through a thicket of twigs. I hunched my shoulders, sure that any second, my head would be bashed in.

Then Brianna tripped. I fell on top of her. And the tips of some falling branches lashed over us. I waited to be crushed.

The roar lessened until it was just a clatter of twigs. Then, just clouds of leaves. We lay there, hardly able to breathe. I thought my heart would jack-hammer right through my chest.

"Brianna, are you okay?" I whispered.

"Yes. How about you?" Her voice shook.

"Fine." I sneezed as the dust settled around us. "I'll get these branches off me and then I'll get off you."

"Okay." I could feel her trembling.

"We're okay, Brianna. We're okay." Gently, I brushed her hair back and tucked it behind her ear. Then I pushed myself up, shoving the branches out of the way and holding them back. I held out my hand to her and she grabbed it. I pulled her up and very quietly, very carefully, we crept out of that forest. Finally, we reached the sunlight.

Somehow I'd forgotten to let go of Brianna's hand. As we walked along the winding trail towards home, our shoulders sometimes nudged each other. Brianna smelled so good — like baby powder and some kind of flower, maybe honeysuckle. A little like eucalyptus dust too.

When we reached the road, we stopped. "I better go home or Mom will fuss," Brianna said.

"I'll walk you home." I reached out to pluck a leaf out of her hair.

So I walked Brianna Santos home, holding her hand like it was the most natural thing in the whole entire universe.

"See you tomorrow," I told her and squeezed her hand gently.

She nodded and gave me the gift of that smile that tumbled my heart over and over.

For a second, we just stood there. I knew what I wanted to do, but as usual, I chickened out.

"Bye, Alex." Brianna headed across the field to her house.

I started towards home. But as I walked away from Brianna, my feet began to drag. They stopped. I looked over my shoulder and, before I knew what I was doing,

I found myself running with huge leaps through the grass, running to catch up to Brianna.

"Wait," I called, breathless. I reached out and cupped her wide-eyed face in my hands. I kissed her right in the middle of her forehead. And I knew instantly and definitely, that, no matter what, I would never ever in my life find a kiss as special as that amazing, fleeting press of my lips on the face of Brianna Santos.

As I floated home, I felt so fine. Even my heinie felt fine. I whistled one of Mom's unbearably happy tunes. Finally, I began belting it out. "Zippa-dee doo-da, zippa-dee aye! My, oh my, what a wonderful day! Plenty of sunshine coming my way, Zippa-dee doo-da, zippa-dee aye!"

I drifted down our driveway and spotted Nic. He was hunched under the curly willow, peering down at the little gimpy chick. His skinny shoulder blades poked out and his hair feathered out in wild wisps. You know, the Albert Einstein Tweety Bird look.

"Hi, Alex!" he called. "I don't have the flu anymore. I'm just fine."

"I know you are, Nic. You are perfectly fine."

He squinted at me like I'd said something strange. Then he turned back to the chick. "Look at this guy." He stroked it with a careful finger. "He's doing great."

I peered at it. It spun in circles, hopping and dragging its bum leg. I felt dizzy watching. "Uhhh..." I frowned.

Then, spotting an ant, it pecked eagerly.

"See, Alex? No worries!" Nic chirped.

"Yeah, I guess you're right." I smiled at him.

"Of course, I'm right!"

"Of course." I rolled my eyes. "Hey, Nic, feel like a bike-ride?"

After a moment of shocked silence, Nic leaped to his feet. "Sure!"

I tilted my bike, swung my leg over it, and stood on my toes, careful not to let my sore seat touch the bike seat. "Come on, then, hop on!"

Nic's whole face smiled as he scrambled aboard. He perched on the seat and hung on to my waist band. His dangling feet jiggled in excitement.

"Hang on!" I stomped down on the pedals and took off, pumping like a maniac. We streaked around the driveway, building momentum for the hill, then we blasted up the slope. Near the top, we almost stalled out, but I gritted my teeth and we made it. In a second, we were soaring down the road, the wind fresh in our faces.

"Yeehaaa! We're flying!" Nic shouted.

"We are, Nic! We're definitely flying!"

We hooted and screeched until we were hoarse. I'd never felt so high in my life.

Later that afternoon, I eased down onto the couch and drowsed off in a nano-second. I must have slept for hours because when I woke up, the sky was dark and the clock was booming over and over. Midnight. I looked out the window and saw the stars glittering. That midnight star called to me. I staggered outside and leaned against the porch railing. It seemed not long ago when I'd wished that things would be different. It was clear to me now, clear as that star blazing in the blackness of the midnight sky, that the thing that was different was me.

Author's Note

Autism is a condition that not only affects the individual, but the whole family. Siblings may need emotional support and a safe place to express their feelings. Organizations that offer support for siblings are listed in the following pages.

Resources for Families and Siblings

Further Reading

Davies, J. (1995) *Able Autistic Children – Children with Asperger's Syndrome: a booklet for brothers and sisters.* London: Mental Health Foundation.

Featherstone, H. (1981) *A Difference in the Family: Living with a Disabled Child.* New York: Viking Press.

Harris, S. and Glasberg, B. (2003) *Siblings of Children with Autism: A Guide for Families.* Bethseda: Woodbine House.

Lobato, D. (1990) *Brothers, Sisters, and Special Needs: Information and Activities for Helping Young Sibings of Children with Chronic Illness and Development Disabilities.* Baltimore: Paul H. Brookes Publishing Company.

Meyer, D. (ed) (1997) *Views from Our Shoes: Growing Up with a Brother or Sister with Special Needs.* Bethseda: Woodbine House.

Meyer, D. and Vadasy, P. (1994) *Sibshops: Workshops for Siblings of Children with Special Needs.* Baltimore: Paul H. Brookes Publishing Company.

Meyer, D. and Vadasy, P. (1996) *Living with a Brother or Sister with Special Needs: A Book for Sibs.* Seattle: University of Washington Press.

Powers, M.D. (2000) *Children with Autism: A Parent's Guide.* Bethseda: Woodbine House.

Siegel, B. and Silverstein, S. (1994) *What About Me? Growing Up with a Developmentally Disabled Sibling.* New York: Plenum Press.

Useful Organizations

Parents Helping Parents – A wonderful organization serving families with exceptional children. Runs support groups, workshops, seminars, and maintains a great library. (www.php.com)

ParentBooks – Stocks over 15,000 titles of interest to families and professionals. (parentbk@netcom.ca)

Siblings Australia Inc. (www.wch.sa.gov.au/sibling/books_mainframe.html)

SibNet – Online support group. (www.seattlechildrens.org/parents/sibsupp.htm)

Buster and the Amazing Daisy

Nancy Ogaz

Daisy White was not crazy. Clumsy maybe, but definitely not crazy. In this exciting adventure story, Daisy, who has autism, defeats her bullies and overcomes her fears with the help of Buster, a very special rabbit. All is going well until a terrible fate threatens Daisy's new friend Cody. Will Daisy be able to gather her courage and special talents to save him? *Buster and the Amazing Daisy* is not just a humorous and engaging story. It will also give its readers an insight into the hopes and dreams, as well as the fears and frustrations, of many children with autism.

'I chose to read this book because the girl in the story is very much like me. And she goes through a lot of the same things I go through every day!'

— Mark Root, Aspie

ISBN 1 84310 721 X

Haze

Kathy Hoopmann

'An absorbing and intriguing story that highlights the strengths and weaknesses of a teenage aspie perfectly...and believe me I should know!'

– Luke Jackson, author of **Freaks, Geeks and Asperger Syndrome: A User Guide to Adolescence**

Seb is a loner. Brilliant with numbers but hopeless with people, he prefers the company of computers and his only friend, Guzzle. Things change for the better when he makes friends with Kristie, Madeline and Jen, and a new computer teacher – Miss Adonia – arrives. However, Seb is soon caught up in a web of computer fraud and lies and turns to Madeline's mysterious cyber friend for help.

Weaving the facts of Asperger Syndrome into the story, this fast-paced book is acclaimed author Kathy Hoopmann's best novel yet and will be a riveting read for teenagers of all sorts and abilities.

Kathy Hoopmann lives in Australia with her husband and three children. She is also the author of the Asperger Adventure series for younger children, *Blue Bottle Mystery, Of Mice and Aliens,* and *Lisa and the Lacemaker,* all published by Jessica Kingsley Publishers.

ISBN 1 84310 072 X